Development Centre Seminars

Globalisation, Poverty and Inequality

Edited by

Richard Kohl

OECD

DEVELOPMENT CENTRE OF THE ORGANISATION
FOR ECONOMIC CO-OPERATION AND DEVELOPMENT

ORGANISATION FOR ECONOMIC CO-OPERATION AND DEVELOPMENT

Pursuant to Article 1 of the Convention signed in Paris on 14th December 1960, and which came into force on 30th September 1961, the Organisation for Economic Co-operation and Development (OECD) shall promote policies designed:

– to achieve the highest sustainable economic growth and employment and a rising standard of living in member countries, while maintaining financial stability, and thus to contribute to the development of the world economy;
– to contribute to sound economic expansion in member as well as non-member countries in the process of economic development; and
– to contribute to the expansion of world trade on a multilateral, non-discriminatory basis in accordance with international obligations.

The original member countries of the OECD are Austria, Belgium, Canada, Denmark, France, Germany, Greece, Iceland, Ireland, Italy, Luxembourg, the Netherlands, Norway, Portugal, Spain, Sweden, Switzerland, Turkey, the United Kingdom and the United States. The following countries became members subsequently through accession at the dates indicated hereafter: Japan (28th April 1964), Finland (28th January 1969), Australia (7th June 1971), New Zealand (29th May 1973), Mexico (18th May 1994), the Czech Republic (21st December 1995), Hungary (7th May 1996), Poland (22nd November 1996), Korea (12th December 1996) and the Slovak Republic (14th December 2000). The Commission of the European Communities takes part in the work of the OECD (Article 13 of the OECD Convention).

The Development Centre of the Organisation for Economic Co-operation and Development was established by decision of the OECD Council on 23rd October 1962 and comprises twenty-two member countries of the OECD: Austria, Belgium, Canada, the Czech Republic, Denmark, Finland, France, Germany, Greece, Iceland, Ireland, Italy, Korea, Luxembourg, Mexico, the Netherlands, Norway, Portugal, Slovak Republic, Spain, Sweden, Switzerland, as well as Chile since November 1998 and India since February 2001. The Commission of the European Communities also takes part in the Centre's Advisory Board.

The purpose of the Centre is to bring together the knowledge and experience available in member countries of both economic development and the formulation and execution of general economic policies; to adapt such knowledge and experience to the actual needs of countries or regions in the process of development and to put the results at the disposal of the countries by appropriate means.

The Centre is part of the "Development Cluster" at the OECD and enjoys scientific independence in the execution of its task. As part of the Cluster, together with the Centre for Co-operation with Non-Members, the Development Co-operation Directorate, and the Sahel and West Africa Club, the Development Centre can draw upon the experience and knowledge available in the OECD in the development field.

 THE OPINIONS EXPRESSED AND ARGUMENTS EMPLOYED IN THIS PUBLICATION ARE THE SOLE RESPONSIBILITY OF THE AUTHOR AND DO NOT NECESSARILY REFLECT THOSE OF THE OECD OR THE GOVERNMENTS OF ITS MEMBER COUNTRIES.

*
* *

Publié en français sous le titre :
Mondialisation, pauvreté et inégalité

© OECD 2003

Foreword

This book is the result of a research programme entitled New Approaches to Poverty Reduction in Development which aimed to combine the knowledge of the OECD Member countries with the experience of poor countries in order to seek the most equitable solutions to the challenges posed by globalisation.

Acknowledgements

The OECD Development Centre wishes to thank the Ford Foundation and the Government of Switzerland for their financial support for the research project on "Income Distribution and Global Interdependence" in the context of which this study was carried out.

Table of Contents

Preface

Over the last 15 years there has been rapidly increasing integration of countries into the world economy — to levels not seen since the early 1990s. Given the simultaneous re-emergence of globalisation and widespread adoption of market reforms, this has led to an intense debate over their effects on national and global poverty, inequality and social exclusion. Is globalisation part of the problem, or part of the solution? On the one hand, globalisation, potentially, provides an opportunity for increased income growth for developing countries which has generally been found to be a necessary pre-condition for reducing poverty. On the other hand, without appropriate national governance, globalisation may increase income inequality between countries and within developing countries. Since there is no reason to believe that globalisation is either systematically good or bad for income inequality and poverty, capturing the effects of globalisation on growth, poverty and inequality in specific instances is essential to understanding why outcomes have been better in some countries than in others.

Globalisation — defined as both greater external integration of national economies and an increased role of markets domestically — began in the 1980s and has largely been driven by multilateral and national policy reforms, rather than technological change, as it was in the last period of intense globalisation. Many developing countries have adopted policies of liberalising trade and capital account flows combined with domestic privatisation and deregulation. These reforms have been based on a fundamental shift in strategy from state-led import substitution philosophy to a market-oriented, export-led approach to development, often in the context of stabilisation and structural adjustment programmes under the pressure of the IMF and the World Bank. Thus questions about the effects of globalisation itself have called into question the role of these institutions in developing countries, and indeed the whole nature of the existing system of global governance, and whose interests it serves. What are the appropriate national development policies to achieve pro-poor globalisation, and what are the implications for global governance?

This volume is based on the papers and discussion drawn from a Development Centre policy dialogue which was held from 30 November to 1 December 2000. This work follows a long line of research and policy dialogues that the Centre has undertaken on various components of globalisation and on inequality and poverty including seminal work on the impact of the Uruguay Round reforms on developing countries, and on the impact of greater openness on skill differentials in the same countries. Recent research has focused on the effects of capital account and financial market liberalisation in various regions in developing countries, particularly the role of different types of foreign capital inflows on growth. Work on globalisation and inequality continued in the Centre's 2001-2002 work programme on "Globalisation and Governance" which was discussed at the Centre's new Governing Board at technical level on 17 March. This includes studies of how to strengthen a process of "inclusive globalisation" in developing countries and emerging markets by accelerating the acquisition of skills and the strengthening of democratic governance.

The results presented in this volume build not only on the Centre's research experience but also on its long tradition of policy dialogue between experts, policy makers and stakeholders. This particular dialogue expanded the participation by stakeholders from developing countries and gave a greater voice to those countries and people in the world economy who do not normally participate in the meetings of international institutions. Their participation shed new light on our understanding of the effects of globalisation from the experience on the ground, improved the quality of the analysis of globalisation and allowed for a more appropriate policy response.

The conclusion of the meeting was that in fact globalisation is not the major cause of income inequality and poverty in developing countries, but that it has contributed to the poor performance in terms of both growth and poverty reduction in a large number of countries. What has differentiated winners from losers both across and within countries has been that globalisation has favoured those countries already well endowed with skills and infrastructure and closely connected to OECD markets. Within countries it has amplified the effects of pre-existing inequalities in the distribution of assets, especially human capital, and in access of the poor to infrastructure and other productive resources. It has magnified the impact of weaknesses in domestic governance and institutions.

This analysis has generated several lessons which are useful for all those involved in development policy, in international institutions, OECD member governments and most of all developing countries. For globalisation to be pro-poor, it needs to be combined with policies which create a more equal distribution of, or access to, productive assets and resources and which build the capacity of vulnerable groups to face successfully increased competition which comes with globalisation. Creating a more equal distribution of human capital through education, training and labour market policies is particularly important. The speed and sequencing of external and domestic liberalisation must be tailored to the particular circumstances of individual countries, based on their institutional capacity to transform the economy. Where institutions and governance are weak, they must be reinforced so that the benefits of globalisation can benefit even the vulnerable parts of populations and the least developed countries. Changes in OECD policies are also necessary; developing countries need increased market access for their exports, especially as regards barriers to primary products and labour-intensive manufactured goods.

Jorge Braga de Macedo
President
OECD Development Centre
27 March 2003

PART ONE

INTRODUCTION
AND A THEORETICAL ORIENTATION

Introduction

Richard Kohl

This volume reflects the outcomes of papers and discussions at an OECD policy dialogue on globalisation held in early December 2000. It focuses on the effects of economic globalisation on poverty and inequality in developing countries, specifically those in Latin America, Southeast Asia and sub-Saharan Africa.

Definitions: Globalisation, Poverty and Inequality

Globalisation, poverty and inequality have become terms so ubiquitous and even ambiguous that it is necessary to start with their definition. While some use "globalisation" to refer to the homogenisation of world culture or the spread of Western or American ideas or even imperialism, that is not the sense used here. This volume considers globalisation in its economic sense. Narrowly defined, this means the greater integration of national economies into the world economy. It involves both processes and outcomes. The processes are policy reforms — trade and capital account liberalisation — and technological change, such as cheaper and better telecommunications and information technology. The proximate outcomes are lower barriers to international flows of goods, capital, labour, technology and ideas that ultimately result in the greater integration of local, regional and national economies into the global market. Local economies become more sensitive to and are more affected by international forces.

This may be the correct definition, but this volume uses a slightly broader one, which refers to the increased role of domestic and international market forces in determining the allocation of goods and services, investment and production and broad socio-economic outcomes. This expanded definition includes domestic policy reforms such as privatisation and deregulation. It corresponds more closely with that used in most policy discussions of globalisation and with reality on the ground in most developing countries. While one can in principle have external or domestic opening without the other, as a matter of fact over the last 20 years they usually have been implemented together as parts of broad policy reform packages, such as structural adjustment and stabilisation programmes under agreements with the Bretton Woods institutions. These packages have most often explicitly targeted moving away from state-led, import-substitution models towards a more market-oriented approach, the so-called Washington consensus. Including domestic market reforms also has an analytical justification. They tend to work synergistically with external opening to multiply the effects of global forces on individual countries and communities. Liberalisation of domestic financial markets can substantially increase the impact of capital account liberalisation, and separating the effects of each component is nearly impossible.

There is growing agreement within the international development community that inequality and poverty must be seen as multi-dimensional, including not just income but also individuals' health, nutrition, and even civil rights and political freedoms. These papers sometimes include other indicators of well-being but, largely for reasons of brevity, generally use the more narrow income definitions of poverty, $1 or $2 per day per person, the measures now embedded in international targets of halving income poverty by 2015. Income inequality is usually measured with gini coefficients, upper to lower quartile/quintile/decile ratios and other statistical measures to summarise inequality within an entire population with a single number.

Developments in Globalisation

Globalisation has become an important policy issue for several reasons. As a process, it has accelerated substantially since the 1980s, particularly for developing countries, driven largely by trade (current account) and capital account liberalisation and, as noted above, domestic reforms including privatisation and a general retreat of the state from direct ownership and intervention in the economy. As a result, globalisation as an outcome has increased. Most developing countries now face more intense international competition (and often greater opportunities), with larger proportions of their economies subject to market forces, particularly international ones. Markets now play a greater role in determining domestic economic, social and cultural outcomes than they did 20 years ago.

The increased role of market forces, or globalisation, has occurred simultaneously with several negative developments. The most dramatic were in the transition countries, where incomes fell very sharply as reforms began to bite, the effects of the monetary overhang generated inflation and CMEA trade collapsed. Then came the Mexican peso crisis of 1994-95 and its contagion effects on the rest of Latin America, the East Asian crisis of 1997 and its contagion effects, and the Russian crisis. A slowdown in global growth accompanied the rising frequency of crises. As the table below shows, growth rates in low-income countries and most regions fell below those attained in 1988-91, becoming negative in Africa. At the same time, reducing the absolute number of people in poverty stagnated or reversed, particularly in Latin America and sub-Saharan Africa, even though the headcount ratio had fallen.

Table 1. **Growth Rates of Per Capita GDP, 1985-98**
(Average annual change, percentages)

Developing Regions	1985-88	1988-91	1991-94	1995-98
Low-Income	9.1	3.1	5.8	1.5
Latin America	4.9	0.5	3.9	0.4
Sub-Saharan Africa	5.2	0.0	1.2	-1.1
East Asia	10.5	5.0	7.4	1.0
South Asia	7.9	2.3	4.1	1.2

Source: GDP Figures are from the World Bank, in current US dollars converted at PPP exchange rates.

By the 1990s these developments led to a perception of rising inequality between countries and increasing social exclusion within them, in the sense of insufficient progress, at best, towards poverty reduction in most countries outside China and East Asia. In some countries absolute poverty was increasing. In the United States, extensive deregulation begun in the mid-1970s was followed by steadily widening wage and income inequality. This generated an intense debate over whether correlation implied causation. Were growing inequality and stagnation of incomes at the bottom due to the effects of the simultaneous globalisation process? As globalisation spread, these same questions were posed regarding poverty and inequality in developing countries and in the world economy writ large. Concern over the effects of globalisation led to a reassessment in development policy circles of the efficacy of a pro-globalisation development strategy, particularly in delivering poverty reduction.

Summarising the various sides of the intellectual and public debate lies beyond the scope of this introduction, especially since there is no consensus view, even among critics. In brief, proponents of globalisation argue that it provides an opportunity for increased income growth and cite evidence that greater openness correlates with greater growth, while there is no correlation, negative or positive, with changes in poverty or inequality. For them, globalisation, especially in the form of domestic liberalisation, has eliminated rents and increased transparency, undermining the economic and political power of privileged groups. Again, they cite evidence linking openness with greater political accountability and democracy[1].

The more critical or nuanced views of globalisation vary and are more difficult to summarise. Perhaps the most modest critique is that trade liberalisation is generally good for growth but that it can often require complementary supply-side and social policies to achieve equitable growth[2]. A broader critique sees no connection between growth and openness when openness is measured by the policy stance rather than by the outcome. The emphasis on trade liberalisation itself is misplaced — the correlation between increased trade and openness and more rapid growth is not causal. Rather, both increased trade and increased growth are joint products of sound institutional and governance frameworks, not a result of reducing policy barriers to trade. With capital account and financial liberalisation, Reisen and others argue that while FDI is generally stable and has a positive impact on growth, short-term capital flows and domestic financial market liberalisation can be destabilising, especially if there is inadequate governance[3]. A still more critical view states that this is precisely the point — capital account liberalisation imposed on countries despite inadequate governance results in capital flight and currency crises. The countries then are held responsible and suffer the consequences of adjustment. The remedy is seen as better domestic governance rather than changing the global governance system that pushes for such policies while failing to provide adequate global regulation and transparency.

Finally, critics question not only the strategy of globalisation, but also its corresponding view on poverty reduction, that poverty in all its various forms could be reduced by increased growth. Instead, the emerging view focuses on the concept of pro-poor growth. In this concept, the effects of growth on poverty depend on the type of growth, emphasis on rural areas is preferable, and markets left to their own devices may not generate that type of result. Growth may be necessary but is not sufficient for lowering poverty, especially when the broader, multi-dimensional definition is used. Complementary social and supply-side policies may be necessary, ranging from social welfare systems to various types of investment to increase the productive capacity of the poor[4]. Bilateral and multilateral development institutions have increasingly adopted this new approach, focusing on attacking poverty directly. The World Bank has recast its own definition and now focuses primarily on poverty reduction. In a number of international forums the community has committed itself to reducing all poverty in its various forms, most importantly halving the number of people in the world living on less than one US dollar per day by 2015.

Perhaps more important than the intellectual debate within development policy circles and international institutions, and certainly more visible in the media, has been the emergence of a popular anti-globalisation movement. It staged a series of public demonstrations against corporate globalisation, beginning at the World Trade Organisation (WTO) negotiations in Seattle in 2000. The variety of criticism of globalisation here is even more diverse, less consistent and difficult to summarise than that found in policy circles. The critiques vary especially between the assorted Northern and Southern versions. Nonetheless, general agreement exists on several common points. Popular critics of globalisation argue that in its current form globalisation is driven by the needs of OECD national governments and multilateral agencies. Consciously or not, they really serve the interests of large multinational financial institutions and corporations (MNEs). Their primary goal is to open up developing country markets so that MNEs can exploit them, rather than by a desire to promote pro-poor growth and sustainable (i.e. environmentally friendly) economic development. For these critics, the result is "corporate globalisation", which increases social exclusion and income inequality both within and across countries. Trade liberalisation causes substantial displacement of labour and hurts workers, small enterprises and import-competing sectors, which do not have access to modern technology, training and infrastructure, or access to sufficient finance to upgrade their skills and equipment. Foreign investment, privatisation and financial market liberalisation have similar effects; they hurt the vulnerable and favour those who already have advantages in asset ownership and access to resources[5].

For the anti-corporate globalisation movement, there are similar negative political effects. Globalisation leads to growing inequality in the distribution of political power both globally and within developing countries. It is most often imposed on developing countries through their agreements with the Bretton Woods institutions, which undermine national sovereignty[6]. Under these programmes countries have no choice but to adopt liberal policies or risk being cut off from international capital flows and, effectively, world markets. This inequity gets mirrored in decision making within international institutions and in the nature of multilateral negotiations as well. The world trade rounds, for example, are seen as strongly biased towards rich countries and their corporate economic interests, not towards Northern workers or Southern countries, let alone the poor within the South.

Domestically, and in marked contrast to the claims of proponents, globalisation is seen as undermining democracy, transparency and accountability. Agreements reached between domestic and international technocrats leave little or no role for legislative debate or approval, as with the "fast-track" approach used to approve trade agreements in the United States. Public political debate or the participation of domestic stakeholders is even more limited. This occurs even when domestic concerns propel liberalisation or it has what is more and more frequently referred to as a high component of domestic ownership. The resulting impact on the economy shifts economic and therefore domestic political power away from relatively immobile factors such as low-skilled labour, SMEs and local and national governments towards that of international capital and highly mobile skilled workers. Thus globalisation shifts the balance of domestic political power towards groups that benefit from it and becomes self-reinforcing, depriving vulnerable parts of the population of effective recourse through the political system.

The OECD Development Centre Dialogue on Globalisation, Poverty and Inequality

In the context of these competing claims about globalisation, the OECD Development Centre organised a dialogue on the effects of globalisation on poverty and inequality (see Appendix I for the programme). The focus was twofold. First, what effects has globalisation had on poverty, inequality and social exclusion in developing countries and by what mechanisms are the effects transmitted? Second, what is the appropriate way for developing countries to integrate into the global economy in order to reduce income inequality and poverty and what does this imply for policy?

To ground the dialogue in a solid, empirical basis of what is in fact happening to developing countries, the Centre commissioned a set of papers to summarise the existing state of knowledge on globalisation. It decided to use a case-study approach, to allow for the evaluation of the variety of experience of individual countries and regions and of relative successes and failures, rather than to focus on the average as implicit in the use of cross-country panel econometric studies[7]. This methodology permitted an assessment of why globalisation improves growth and reduces poverty more in some countries than others and perhaps even hurts some countries absolutely. It enabled policy recommendations on what could be done to increase the number of positive outcomes[8].

The Centre commissioned studies of ten developing countries in sub-Saharan Africa, Southeast Asia and Latin America[9] and a set of six regional papers, two for each region, analysing how and why the social impact of globalisation, *ex post*, varied across countries in the regions. To provide the global context, the Centre also commissioned four background papers on global trends in inequality and poverty and their relationship to globalisation, including one by Centre staff. (See Appendix II for a list of the papers.)

The design of the dialogue gave equal weight to the concerns of both OECD countries and developing country participants, especially representatives of civil society. The participation of Southern stakeholders was key to achieving the substantive goals of the dialogue. Their perspective, from experience on the ground, would shed a new and different light on our understanding of the effects of globalisation, improve the quality of the analysis and allow for a more appropriate policy response. Moreover, in the context of Seattle and the anti-globalisation movement, the Centre wanted to include countries and people in the world economy that do not normally participate in the meetings of international institutions. It wanted to give them an opportunity to describe their experience and to give the representatives of the institutions and OECD country governments an opportunity to listen, learn and respond. In the event, the stakeholders from developing countries participated very actively and their participation led to a much better sense of the objections to globalisation, especially given the findings of the background papers (see Appendix III for a list of participants).

The general conclusion of the papers and discussion was that globalisation contributes to unsatisfactory outcomes in many developing countries, but the net effects are small. It has had both positive and negative effects, often minor and offsetting each other. In other words, globalisation is not the major source of development problems or poverty and inequality; domestic factors are much more important. Nevertheless, in many of the countries discussed at the meeting, globalisation in its current form makes pre-existing problems of domestic origin worse, negatively affecting the least developed countries and the most vulnerable groups in all developing countries (the poor, farmers, workers, small businesses and particularly women). An even larger share of developing populations may not be worse off in an absolute sense, and may even be better off, but is largely excluded from participating in the benefits of globalisation. These people are left behind, and the result is wider social and economic inequality. Both of these effects come from insufficient attention to preparing domestic economies for greater competition.

The dialogue identified four areas needing domestic policy to remedy this neglect: governance and institutions; capacity building, such as education and training; providing access to markets (through infrastructure, particularly communication); and better redistributive policy through social safety nets. It concluded that domestic policy reforms cannot be effective without international support. A number of international institutions, especially the World Bank, IMF and WTO, must become more inclusive and adopt policies that better serve the interests of developing countries. Better representation of stakeholders in international institutions and at international negotiations would facilitate the explicit adoption of pro-poor, pro-development policies.

Notes

1. In this view trade liberalisation results in lower prices that benefit consumers and can stimulate overall growth through increased demand and improvements in productivity due to specialisation, greater access to technology and capital and creation of dynamic efficiency. A new body of literature is even emerging that argues that trade openness causes better governance, such as less corruption. Similar arguments are made for the positive roles of capital inflows, FDI, privatisation and deregulation.

2. Perhaps the most influential proponent of the moderate view has been Alan Winters. See Winters (1999). Subsequent versions have appeared as working papers by the UK development agency, DFID.

3. Reisen and Soto (2001) find that FDI and portfolio equity flows exert strong independent growth effects while short-term debt has negative independent growth effects if domestic banking systems are undercapitalised.

4. See the literature cited in the OECD DAC Poverty Reduction Guidelines (2001), for example.

5. FDI is concentrated in natural resources or export zones with little domestic content or backward linkages into the domestic economy, or increasingly in more modern sectors like financial services where it benefits only highly educated workers. Similarly, privatisation and deregulation result in substantial shedding of low-skilled workers, loss of universal, affordable services, especially to vulnerable parts of the population, and the emergence of for-profit monopolies charging higher prices.

6. Because the North ultimately dominates the institutions' agendas through their boards of directors, they have pushed a "one-size-fits-all" model of development. Little attention is paid to institution building or social policies, and trade liberalisation has become an end in itself rather than a means to achieve growth, development or equity.

7. It has become quite popular in the economic development literature to look at the effects of globalisation on growth, inequality and poverty by using econometric techniques to analyse cross-country data. These approaches have often found conflicting or little evidence of any link between globalisation and poverty or inequality. Even if there is no systematic correlation, however, this does not mean that globalisation has no effect, but rather that it may be making things worse in some countries and better in others. See the various papers by Dollar and Kraay and their ongoing debate with Dani Rodrik. A recent version is Dollar and Kraay (2001).

8. This theme is expanded upon in the transcript of the GCARs talk included in this volume (Part Five).

9. Initially the regions to be included in the dialogue were middle-income countries from Latin America and Southeast Asia rather than the low-income countries of Southeast Asia and sub-Saharan Africa. In the event it was decided to include sub-Saharan African countries precisely because they had been largely left out of much of the change in globalisation and to see if there might be insights from middle-income countries which could be applied there.

Bibliography

DOLLAR, D and A. KRAAY (2001), "Trade, Growth and Poverty", mimeo, Development Research Group, World Bank, Washington, D.C., January.

OECD DEVELOPMENT ASSISTANCE COMMITTEE (DAC) (2001), *Poverty Reduction Guidelines*, OECD, Paris.

REISEN, H. and M. SOTO (2001), "Which Types of Capital Inflows Foster Developing-Country Growth?", *International Finance*, Vol. 4, No. 1.

WINTERS, L.A. (1999), "Trade and Poverty, Is there a Connection?", Chapter 3 *in* H. NORDSTROM (ed.) *Trade, Income and Poverty*, WTO, Geneva.

Globalisation and Endogenous Educational Responses: The Main Economic Transmission Channels

François Bourguignon[1] and Thierry Verdier[2]

Introduction

Globalisation now clearly is a widespread and unavoidable phenomenon for national economies. It affects countries through various channels: trade or financial liberalisation, foreign direct investment, multinationalisation of firms and technology transfers. While it generates undoubtedly important aggregate economic gains to the world economy and to national economies, it nevertheless has been strongly questioned because of its potentially adverse effects on income distribution and inequality. Indeed, it has been associated by many observers with, for instance, the noticeable increase in wage or unemployment inequality between skilled and unskilled workers observed since the 1980s in several industrial and emerging economies. A rapidly growing literature has started to identify channels through which deeper international integration might eventually affect income inequality and unemployment. Two important aspects have generally been opposed in this line of research: skill-biased technological change (Berman, Bound and Griliches, 1994; Lawrence and Slaughter, 1993; Krugman, 1995) and growing international trade integration (Wood, 1994; Leamer, 1994; Rodrik, 1997; Feenstra and Hanson, 1999)[3].

Most of this analysis is static in the sense that it focuses on wage differentials across various skills given by individual characteristics. One potentially important channel not much investigated is the acquisition of human capital or more specifically the educational response to globalisation by national economies and governments. The contrasted examples of East Asian and Latin American economies in this respect suggest that such a channel may exist and help explain the diversity of country experiences.

This paper presents a first discussion of how globalisation can generate different domestic educational responses in developing economies and the corresponding implications for the political economy of education and its associated redistributive conflicts. Given the lack of empirical studies to date on these issues, the approach is exploratory and mainly theoretical. A little reflection also suggests that the links between globalisation and domestic educational responses are numerous and complex. Discussing them in one single integrative framework seems a daunting task and not necessarily a useful exercise for interesting insights on these issues. Instead of this comprehensive approach, the paper considers a variety of simplified archetypal models of a small, open-developing economy. It investigates how the results derived from the literature on trade and human capital can be incorporated into the recent literature on the political economy of education and development, hitherto concerned mainly with closed economies.

The discussion is mostly speculative. Its main objective is to identify the nature of the various channels through which external liberalisation may affect educational behaviour and the accumulation of human capital. No attempt is made for the moment to test the empirical relevance of each of them, fundamentally because of a lack of data. The links analysed are indirect and take time to materialise. Trying to disentangle them from other determinants of the evolution of the educational level of a population requires in-depth case studies of a sample of countries. Standard cross-country comparisons are simply of no use in this matter, and embarking on detailed comparative country studies was much beyond the paper's scope. One may hope that the discussion will provide incentives for such research.

An important feature of developing economies is that they are prone to many market failures. A relevant analysis of the channels through which globalisation affects educational responses has to take this into account at least to some extent. The paper focuses on the role of credit markets and more generally asset market imperfections. It discusses the role of liquidity constraints and their macroeconomic implications for investment in human capital, but leaves aside other market imperfections that may be equally salient. These include imperfections in the labour and goods markets and the impact of their institutional characteristics on domestic educational responses[4]. While their effects are potentially important, they lie beyond the scope of the paper and await future research.

Political Economy Considerations of External Liberalisation and Redistribution

The standard efficiency view in any international economics textbook suggests that external liberalisation generates substantial gains for an economy. A well-known economic argument for developing countries holds that the rate of return to capital is higher than in the rest of the world. Opening up to capital flows thus should make the economy more efficient. The same argument often justifies liberalising goods markets.

Adjusting to world prices permits increasing the total surplus in the economy. Similarly, technology transfers and foreign direct investment create opportunities to reap productivity gains at the national level. If the appropriate redistribution mechanisms were available, it should then be possible to compensate the losers fully without confiscating all the gains of the gainers.

This "first-best" type of situation often lies far from reality. Developing economies often are subject to failures in labour and asset markets. Serious imperfections may also exist in good markets, and externalities (positive and negative) may be present. Existing local institutions may not adequately compensate for all these sources of inefficiency. If so, second-best theory tells us that there is no longer a presumption that external liberalisation should bring a surplus to the economy. More relevant perhaps from a political-economy point of view, lump-sum transfer mechanisms to redistribute the gains from trade seldom are feasible. Because of asymmetric information or previous commitments, governments must use distortive instruments to redistribute resources across social groups. They destroy the first-best separability between efficiency and distribution. In some cases, the economic distortions introduced by redistribution may be able to dissipate the direct gains from liberalisation.

Several models handling this kind of issue formally in an explicit imperfect-information context have been developed recently (Feenstra, 1987; Lewis, Feenstra and Ware, 1989; Gabaix, 1999; Guesnerie, 1999; Spector, 1999). In this literature, the impossibility of implementing lump-sum transfers rests on the incapacity of the government to distinguish losers from gainers precisely and without cost. Any redistributive scheme has to be "incentive compatible", which implies relying on taxes and subsidies that distort resource allocation to redistribute the gains from liberalisation. Under such constraints, free trade may not be Pareto superior to autarky, and external liberalisation may actually prove immiserising or at least strongly disequalising for some social groups. These kinds of arguments underlie the rapidly expanding literature on endogenous trade protection (Hillman, 1989; Rodrik, 1995), pointing out that external liberalisation may be opposed because it hurts interests of specific social groups that cannot be compensated by simple internal redistributive mechanisms. These issues obviously have crucial importance in the debate on globalisation and income distribution. If, arguably, international integration contributes to dramatic changes in income inequality (notably between skilled and unskilled labour), then, from a political economy perspective, one may expect high pressures on national governments for internal redistribution or, by default, for opposition to external openness. In both cases, this may result in significant dead-weight losses in the national economy.

This view relies on a standard framework where factor endowments are fixed and efficiency is concerned with the allocation of resources. Under these conditions, the question arises whether the same trade-off holds between redistribution and allocative efficiency when the supply of factors is endogenous. As human capital accumulation and education have both distributive and allocative effects, one might expect that policies in this area could help capture the gains from external liberalisation while producing acceptable change or no change in income distribution. In such a perspective, two sets of issues must be considered. First, what are the effects of globalisation or external liberalisation on private incentives to education and human capital accumulation in a decentralised market economy? Does this endogenous educational response exacerbate or mitigate in the medium run the initial impact of international integration on the distribution of income? Second, taking into account public choices in education, how does opening affect the political economy of educational policies? In the medium term, what does this imply for long-run distribution and possibly for the evolution of the political institutions ultimately responsible for mediating redistributive conflicts?

Private Educational Responses to External Liberalisation

What effects does openness have on the supply of skills in an open economy? To consider this question, one has to depart from the standard assumption in international economics that factor endowments are in fixed supply. Various trade models have specifically investigated the issue: (Findlay and Kierzkowski, 1983; Stokey, 1991a, 1991b; and Cartiglia, 1997). Most explored the issue of trade integration. The acquisition of skill or human capital is an investment decision. As is usual when one deals with investment, it is useful to distinguish complete and perfect asset markets from incomplete and/or imperfect ones. Although assuming the first clearly does not offer the most appropriate framework to analyse development issues, it provides a useful benchmark against which to evaluate the effects of the second.

Perfect Asset Markets

When an economy has perfect asset markets, the main determinant of skill accumulation is the relative return to education. This in turn is determined by the evolution of two important factor prices, namely the wage rates of skilled and unskilled workers. The educational response to globalisation is thus tightly associated with the direct impact it has on these factor prices. Globalisation may, of course, involve various channels: trade integration, financial integration, technology transfers and migration. For a small, open-developing economy, one may expect external liberalisation to affect the economy differently according to the channel considered.

Trade Integration. A simple way to start discussing the impact of trade integration on educational responses is to consider a standard Hecksher-Ohlin model of trade with two goods produced using unskilled and skilled labour, where trade is driven mainly by traditional relative factor-endowment differences. The effect of trade on factor rewards then depends on the comparative advantage of the country. A small, open-developing economy relatively abundant in unskilled and relatively scarce in skilled labour will have a comparative advantage in the good that is intensive in unskilled labour and will tend to export that good. The relative wage gap between skilled labour and unskilled labour should thus narrow after trade liberalisation, in accordance with the familiar Stolper-Samuelson theorem. The return to education consequently will also go down. Compared to autarky, trade openness thus tends to depress the incentives to invest in education. The initial pattern of relative factor endowments gets reinforced in the sense that, over time, it tends to become more biased towards a relative abundance of unskilled labour. The immediate endogenous educational response to globalisation tends to accentuate the direct impact of trade integration, reinforcing the comparative advantage structure of the economy[5] [6].

As long as the economy remains unspecialised, the wage gap between skilled and unskilled workers stays at its post-trade-integration level as factor prices are disconnected from factor endowments. Three possibilities can occur in the long run. There may exist a skilled/unskilled wage ratio such that the economy remains unspecialised (1), or the wage gap between skilled and unskilled workers drives the economy to specialisation either in the skill-intensive good (2) or in the unskilled labour intensive good (3). In the last case, factor prices depend again on domestic factor endowments and domestic factor market forces play their stabilising role in the economy.

The conclusion that trade integration implies an educational response accentuating the initial pattern of comparative advantage is also true in other trade contexts. Consider, for instance, a situation in which factors are, at least in the medium run, sector-specific. This is best illustrated by, say, a Ricardo-Viner model with unskilled and skilled labour the sector-specific factors and capital the intersectorally mobile one. Again trade will tend to increase the relative return of the factor specific to the sector in which the country has a comparative advantage. If this turns out to be unskilled (or skilled) labour, then the endogenous educational response will be negative (or positive) and the country's pattern of comparative advantage will again be reinforced.

In the preceding framework where factor prices are not set abroad, the induced change in factor endowments tends to reduce the initial impact of openness on the distribution of income. For example, for a skill-scarce developing economy, trade integration causes a direct decrease in the wage gap between skilled and unskilled labour and less inequality. Yet it also induces a smaller endogenous supply of skilled labour, which will then tend to push up the skilled wage rate and increase the wage gap, although this second effect cannot overcome the direct impact under reasonable stability assumptions. Additionally, the reduction in skilled labour releases the mobile factor, capital, from the sector using it to that using unskilled labour. This strengthens the unskilled wage rate, with further pressure narrowing the wage gap and wage inequality[7].

Introducing Capital Mobility. How would the above conclusions be affected when globalisation occurs through international capital mobility? Consider a developing economy that is capital-poor compared with the rest of the world. Under this condition, the common assumption holds that the return on capital before integration is higher at home than abroad. Financial liberalisation will then induce a capital inflow into the country. As a consequence, it is quite likely that the demand for skilled and unskilled labour will increase, implying an increase in both skilled and unskilled wages. Whether the return on education will increase or not depends on the variation of the wage gap between skilled and unskilled labour. This in turn depends on the technology parameters of the economy, namely the relative degree of complementarity between capital, skilled labour and unskilled labour. If capital is strongly complementary to skilled labour and less so to unskilled labour, as commonly assumed, the wage gap between skilled and unskilled workers will increase, raising inequality and at the same time stimulating domestic incentives to invest in human capital. The induced educational response to capital mobility is therefore positive. The endogenous change in factor endowments should then mitigate the initial impact of international capital mobility on wage inequality.

Technology Transfers. One may similarly analyse the effects of technology transfers. These effects could occur through licensing to domestic producers, foreign direct investment by multinationals or spillovers from trade-embodied technologies. What is important is whether they increase the return to education in the country. Whether in the previous Hecksher-Ohlin setting or in the factor specific framework, clear-cut implications can be derived. In the small, open, Hecksher-Ohlin economy with skilled and unskilled labour mobile across sectors, what matters for the return to education is the sectoral bias of the technology transfer[8]. As a matter of fact, the technology transfer is equivalent to an exogenous change in domestic prices and the Stolper-Samuelsonian theorem on relative factor prices applies. Hence, if technology transfers fall mainly on the skill-intensive sector, the wage gap between skilled and unskilled labour increases, raising inequality but triggering a positive endogenous educational response.

In the Ricardo-Viner model with skilled and unskilled labour sector specific, technology transfers play a role through two channels. Consider again that the technology transfer occurs in the sector using skilled labour as a specific factor. The first effect is the standard partial-equilibrium effect that the technology transfer improves the productivity of the sector, implying, everything else equal, an increase in the price of the factor specific to that sector, namely skilled labour. Second, a general-equilibrium effect works through the market for intersectorally mobile capital. As productivity in the skilled labour sector goes up, its demand for capital increases. This shifts up the return to capital, depressing the return to the factor specific to the other sector, namely unskilled labour. For both reasons, one may then expect technology transfers towards the skill-specific sector to increase the wage gap and therefore the return to education.

Labour Mobility and Brain Drain is the last channel through which globalisation may affect the economy. First, consider again the Hecksher-Ohlin model with skilled and unskilled labour. As long as there is international factor-price equalisation, nothing should happen with labour mobility as domestic skilled and unskilled wages are equalised with those of the rest of the world. Where initial factor-price equalisation does not hold, two possibilities can occur, before migration. Either the economy is specialised in the production of the unskilled-intensive good or it is diversified in the production of both goods but its initial domestic skilled to unskilled labour endowment ratio is in a diversification cone different from that of the rest of the world. Similar conclusions would obtain if there were some barriers to trade. Suppose then, to fix ideas, that only skilled labour migration is possible (brain drain) and that, before migration, the wage of skilled labour in the rest of the world is higher than the domestic one[9]. This obviously stimulates emigration of domestic skilled workers, decreasing the domestic skilled to unskilled labour force ratio in the economy. At the equilibrium, domestic skilled labour wages will equalise with those of the rest of the world. Whether the economy ends up specialising in the production of the unskilled-intensive good or diversified in the production of both goods, the domestic wage gap between skilled and unskilled labour increases. This, in turn, stimulates the incentives to accumulate human capital in the domestic economy. Obviously, this investment in human capital need not increase local production, as newly educated workers will still have an incentive to emigrate.

In the Ricardo-Viner framework with sector-specific skilled and unskilled labour, the implications of migration for domestic educational responses are also quite intuitive. Again, if skilled workers have an incentive to move outside the country because of higher wages in the rest of the world, then at the migration equilibrium, the domestic wage of educated workers is likely to move up to the rest-of-world level. Migration of skilled workers in the skilled labour sector releases physical capital that will move to the unskilled labour sector. This increases the demand for unskilled labour and pushes up the unskilled wage rate. The wage gap between skilled and unskilled labour is still higher than before migration, however. Again, opening foreign labour markets to skilled workers enhances inequality and incentives to invest in education. As before, the long-run impact on relative domestic labour endowments will not favour skilled labour. The brain drain process will continue to ensure that domestic skilled-labour wages remain the same as abroad. More education will essentially feed the brain drain.

Dynamic Trade Models. The preceding discussion considered the effect of external openness on the incentives to invest in human capital essentially through comparative statics exercises on standard static trade models. Dynamic trade models that integrate the process of skill acquisition lead to the same types of conclusions. For example, Findlay and Kierzkowski (1983) embedded the model of human capital accumulation *à la* Mincer in the standard Hecksher-Ohlin model. In a dynamic context they found the basic intuitive result that trade reduces the incentives to accumulate human capital in initially skill-scarce countries. As in the simpler static frameworks, the accumulation of human capital in such countries falls when the return to education is reduced by the penetration of cheaper skill-intensive import goods[10].

Natural Limitations of Empirical Evidence. The empirical evidence that would be relevant to test the various hypotheses discussed so far is twofold. First, the problem is to know whether the skilled/unskilled wage differential has responded in the expected way to the various types of external liberalisation considered. Second, did educational behaviour respond to these incentives in the expected way? Existing evidence is extremely limited on both fronts.

The voluminous literature on the relationship between globalisation and wage differentials mostly concerns developed economies [see Katz and Autor (1999) for example]. It also is rather inconclusive as to whether observed increases in the wage gap result from the extension of international trade, enhanced competition, technological change or other factors (Atkinson, 2000). There also is empirical evidence that the wage gap increased in several developing countries over the last ten to 15 years, but this evolution is far from universal. For instance, wage inequality has increased substantially in several Latin American countries — Brazil, Chile, Colombia, Mexico — but much less in Southeast Asian countries apparently equally concerned with the process of globalisation. The wage structure shrank in Chinese Taipei between 1979 and 1994 and did not show any clear trend in Indonesia. In Thailand and Malaysia, however, some increase in the wage gap was observed in the early 1990s[11], but whether it related to globalisation is quite another story. The few attempts to find a causal relationship between the two phenomena were not successful.

More than for developed countries, the preceding discussion helps an understanding of why such analysis is difficult and why cross-country evidence on the evolution of wage gaps may be contradictory. Trade liberalisation simply is likely to have a different impact on wage inequality from the liberalisation of capital flows or technological transfers from the North. It is quite conceivable that the trade effect has been dominant in a country like Chinese Taipei whereas the technology factor is dominant in Latin America. Disentangling these various effects requires in-depth case studies that go beyond the scope of this paper (See Robbins, 1999).

Whether there generally is a significant educational response to changes in the rate of return to education implied by variations in the skill structure of earnings is equally difficult to determine. Here again, the database that would be necessary to test this hypothesis is missing in most developing countries. The level of human capital in developing countries follows an ascending trend and identifying whether acceleration or deceleration of that trend has been associated with changes in the skill wage differential is practically impossible either on time series or in cross-section data. Moreover, this trend may have changed over time for many other reasons, including a pure income effect, which may depend on credit-market imperfection.

The Role of Imperfect Asset Markets

The previous discussion suggests that trade is likely to provide incentives for amplifying existing endowment differences. For developing economies, which presumably are skill-scarce countries, trade openness tends to depress the wage skill premium and therefore private incentives to education. Capital mobility or technology transfers mitigate this somewhat, under the assumption that they both tend to favour the position of skilled workers. The possibility of skilled labour emigration may also stimulate educational efforts, but without necessarily improving the skill endowment and growth potential of the economy.

All the previous discussion assumes that all markets are perfect — markets for all factors and goods are competitive and clear without friction. Most importantly, all individuals freely borrow as much as they wish to invest in education if they find that profitable. This contrasts starkly with observed reality in most developing countries, where imperfect competition often prevails for economic or institutional reasons in factor and goods markets. Asymmetries of information may generate significant search and screening costs, which prevent these markets from functioning smoothly.

The impact of all these imperfections on the channels through which globalisation affects domestic educational responses presents an important research agenda. This paper concentrates on the role of credit and asset market imperfections, which may prevent people from investing in education even when it would be profitable. Indeed, several studies suggest that credit rationing may be the main obstacle to human capital accumulation in many developing countries (see, for instance, Psacharopoulos and Woodhall, 1985; and Cameron and Heckman, 1990). Liquidity constraints may well modify the main conclusions obtained above. They imply that educational investments are no longer determined solely by how globalisation affects the wage gap or the return to education. They also depend on how changes in domestic prices, induced by external openness, will affect the likelihood for potential investors to be liquidity constrained.

Imperfect Credit Markets. Few studies have considered explicitly the link between international openness and education with missing credit markets. A notable recent exception is Cartiglia (1997). His model and conclusions run in a direction opposite from this paper so far and deserve summary here. The model combines that of the small, open economy with skilled and unskilled labour as specific factors, capital as the mobile factor and an overlapping generation framework. Agents live two periods. They start the first period of their lives with different capital endowments. During this period, they can either go to school or work as unskilled workers. If they opt for schooling, they acquire skills that allow them to work as skilled workers in the second period. At the end of the second period, all individuals die and have one child. The education system is skill intensive in the sense that skilled workers are required to educate individuals who decide to go to school. Education is private and competitively run. Hence, in order to invest in education, individuals have to pay a fixed education fee, which depends positively on the wage rate of skilled labour. At the same time, there is no domestic credit market for education. Therefore, individuals have to finance their educational investment out of the income from their initial capital endowment. It follows that educational decisions are determined by the extent of liquidity constraints faced by individuals in this economy. Poorly endowed individuals cannot finance up-front the fixed cost of education. Only rich enough agents can invest in human capital accumulation. The shape of the distribution of initial endowments in the economy thus determines the pattern of skills[12].

With this model one can investigate the endogenous educational response of further trade integration and contrast it with what would happen without credit-market failures. The striking feature is that, for a country with an initial comparative advantage in the sector employing unskilled labour, trade integration induces a positive educational response. The intuition is simple. The crucial determinant of human capital investment in this economy is the liquidity constraint faced by the marginal individual who decides to invest in education. When there is trade opening, the relative price of the tradable sector using skilled labour is lower compared with autarky. Consequently, the wage rate of skilled labour falls while that of unskilled labour rises. As the education system is skill intensive, this also reduces the equilibrium fee for investment in human capital. This relaxes the liquidity constraint faced by individuals who want to get to school. The number of unskilled agents who get involved in the education system increases, providing in the next period an additional number of educated workers. This increased supply of skilled labour tends to depress the skilled wage rate further, accentuating the initial impact of trade liberalisation and promoting even more education in the next period. The process will stop when the wage gap has been reduced to the point where the return to education, rather than liquidity constraint, becomes the single determinant of education investment.

Two important aspects of the model are responsible for the positive educational response to opening. First, at least for a broad range of changes in the prices of goods due to opening, it is necessary that human capital investment decisions depend crucially on the liquidity constraints faced by poor agents rather than on the wage gap between skilled and unskilled labour. Second, the education system must be skill intensive (through teachers) and should not involve any significant fixed capital cost. If, on the contrary, skilled labour in the education sector is strongly complementary with important capital infrastructure, then the educational response to trade opening can be seriously mitigated. A change in the skilled labour wage will not significantly reduce the cost of education or increase the number of people who become educated[13].

Specific Human Capital, General Human Capital and Mobility. As first noted by Becker (1964), various aspects of human capital are specific to firms and sectors and can increase a worker's productivity only in that context. When markets are incomplete, particularly insurance markets, this feature can have important consequences in a world of uncertainty and stochastic shocks. More precisely, workers undertaking sector-specific human capital investments may face important adjustment costs if they have to move from one sector to another once the uncertainty is resolved. This may affect their incentives to invest in specific education. To the extent that trade and financial integration introduce unpredictable foreign competitive pressures and make the economy subject to external shocks, they may actually increase the uncertainty borne by local workers. This can trigger a negative response in specific human capital investment with detrimental effects on growth. An alternative for workers that becomes more profitable on opening may be to invest in general education to adapt more quickly to changes in the economic environment. By reducing the adjustment costs of inter-sector or inter-firm mobility, general education can be viewed as a partial insurance mechanism that also improves the general productivity of workers. It follows that, whenever openness increases individual uncertainty, it will likely trigger a higher demand for general education and may possibly have positive effects on growth.

A recent paper by Kim and Kim (2000) formally investigates these ideas. The authors consider a multi-sector general-equilibrium model in which industries undergo, in each period, uncertain technological changes that differ across industries and over time. Individuals can invest in two different types of human capital: sector-specific and general. They can acquire specific human capital either through on-the-job-training and job experience or at school, with the help of general human capital. General human capital is obtainable only at school and allows workers to acquire any type of industry-specific human capital. In this sense, general human capital is essential to increase or maintain worker mobility across sectors.

Using this model, the paper looks at the impact of trade integration on the economic growth pattern. In autarky, all goods must be produced domestically. Consequently, the average growth rate of the country depends on the average rate of industrial technical progress. With international trade and general human capital, the economy specialises in the sector with the greatest productivity in each period, implying that growth depends on the technical progress of the sector that progresses fastest. This pushes up the average growth rate. On the other hand, when there is no general human capital and only sector-specific human capital, workers cannot easily move from one sector to another. As a result, the economy cannot fully benefit from the highest technical progress that specialisation would otherwise permit. Average growth depends again on average technical progress across sectors, and international opening no longer improves growth performance. While the authors do not analyse this explicitly, the singular growth performance difference between open economies with and without general education suggests that autonomous trade integration increases the private and social return of general human capital and should therefore imply a positive endogenous response in general education.

Implications for Inequalities and Redistributive Conflicts

The previous sections identified various channels through which external openness can endogenously affect domestic investment in human capital. An important element is the idea that the private educational response to opening depends on whether opening occurs through trade integration or financial and technological integration, and whether there are asset-market failures.

Table 2 presents the effects of globalisation on education incentives (the skilled labour/unskilled labour wage gap) and changes in local factor endowments, according to the various channels considered (trade, capital mobility, technology transfer, labour mobility) and the two archetypal models of a small, open, developing, skill-scarce economy. The first column considers the two-sector Hecksher-Ohlin model with two mobile factors (skilled and unskilled labour). The second column shows the two-sector factor-specific model with skilled and unskilled labour the specific factors and capital the mobile one. All cases distinguish between the effects of perfect asset markets and imperfect credit markets and liquidity constraints on human capital investment (italic), with the implicit assumption that the educational sector is skill intensive in the economy.

Table 2. **A Summary of the Basic Model Results**

Type of External Liberalisation and Credit-Market Assumptions	Two-Sector Trade Models	
	Heckscher-Ohlin Model: Unskilled (U) and Skilled Labour (S) Are Mobile	Factor-Specific Model: Unskilled (U) and Skilled Labour (S) Are Specific, Capital (K) Is Mobile
International trade	- wage gap falls - less education	- wage gap falls - less education
Liquidity constrained:	- *more education*	- *more education*
Capital mobility		- wage gap? - more education when K is strong complement of S
Liquidity constrained:		- *less education* when K is strong complement of S
Technology transfer (complement to skilled labour)	- wage gap increases - more education	- wage gap increases - more education
Liquidity constrained:	- *less education*	- *less education*
Labour mobility (skilled labour)	- wage gap increases - more education	- wage gap increases - more education
Liquidity constrained:	- *less education*	- *less education*
Labour mobility (unskilled labour)	- wage gap falls - less education	- wage gap falls - less education
Liquidity constrained:	- *more education*	- *more education*

When there is no credit market imperfection for the accumulation of human capital, a general conclusion is that trade integration and its implied pattern of specialisation tends to reduce the incentives for individuals to invest in education. With financial integration associated with capital inflows and/or technology transfers, openness, on the contrary, tends to stimulate a positive educational response. The induced educational response, by its subsequent effects on factor endowments, tends to mitigate the initial impact of globalisation on factor prices and in particular on wage inequalities. Labour mobility, depending on whether it facilitates skilled or unskilled workers' migration, has contrasting effects on local educational efforts. The impact on inequality is generally expected to be negative when migration involves skilled workers and positive when it involves unskilled workers.

In the more realistic situation where some individuals face credit market imperfections, the educational response to globalisation does not depend only on the way openness affects market prices but also on how it changes the structure of liquidity constraints within the country. Educational responses to globalisation are then quite different from the case of perfect credit markets. If the education system is mainly skill intensive and if education investments are completely determined by credit rationing, then trade integration will likely stimulate a positive education response[14]. Yet capital inflows, technology transfers and brain drain migration, by raising the skilled labour wage and therefore education fees, may do just the opposite — depress the educational effort of workers. By raising the unskilled labour wage rate, however, the migration of unskilled labour allows unskilled workers to alleviate their liquidity constraint and eventually invest more in human capital.

In terms of social inequalities and associated redistributive conflicts, external integration, whenever it tends to increase the return to education, inevitably enlarges the wage gap between skilled and unskilled labour. When credit markets are perfect, the induced change in factor endowments is partly self-correcting and therefore may alleviate this unequal direct impact of openness and its associated redistributive conflicts. When the economy is subject to serious domestic credit market imperfections, however, a pattern of external integration that increases the gap between skilled and unskilled labour will likely accentuate initial social tensions. The direct unequal impact of some types of liberalisation between skilled and unskilled workers remains as before, but, more important, the induced educational response to integration is now likely to exacerbate it. To the extent that the educational system is skill intensive and that openness increases the relative reward to skilled labour, the up-front cost of education increases. A larger fraction of poor individuals may find themselves liquidity constrained in their skill acquisition while rich agents not liquidity constrained actually gain a higher return on their education investment. In the end, wage inequality is very likely to increase.

One can derive a number of implications in terms of the political economy of opening, redistribution and education for small, open, developing economies. In the realistic case of asset-market failures, external integration, whenever it increases the return to education — through capital inflows and technology transfers — will likely generate important redistributive conflicts. The expression of these conflicts can take three possible forms — protectionist pressures to reduce external openness, pressures to redistribute the gains from trade through fiscal and tax policies and pressures for educational policies, such as subsidies or public provision, which may alleviate the seriousness of credit market constraints. Clearly, the final outcome will depend on the intensity of preferences of the various agents as well as on the nature of political institutions and the distribution of political power in society.

The protectionist and the internal income redistribution avenues have been investigated extensively or revived in the literature on international economics or development. (See Rodrik, 1995, on the political economy of protection; Dixit, 1985, Guesnerie, 1999, and Spector, 1999, on the fiscal redistribution of the gains of trade; and Rodrik, 1998, on domestic social institutions responsible for risk sharing and redistribution.) The third option has remained largely unexplored. The following section discusses it.

Openness and Education: the Political-Economy Channel

The previous section discussed educational responses to increased external integration, taking into account price incentives as well as possible liquidity constraints faced by individuals who would like to get educated. It considered the structure of the "market" educational response to external integration for *given* public policies, in particular for redistribution. In a political economy perspective, however, public policies are the result of public choices, which address redistributive conflicts through the mediation of specific political institutions. Given the large distributive issues associated with the process of human capital accumulation and globalisation, there is no reason to expect public policies in redistribution and/or education to remain fixed under external integration. Therefore, a full description of the educational response to openness should also pay attention to the endogenous public policy responses of governments. One can expect the nature of domestic institutions and the structure of political power to affect the educational response to openness.

Conversely, it is also quite likely that openness, through the domestic changes it generates in human capital accumulation, may have important implications for the nature of the political transition along the development path of the economy. Indeed, a distinctive political-economy feature of education is that, on top of having direct economic effects on productivity and learning, it also has direct effects on the structure of political power within a country. It has been widely acknowledged in political science that education has a positive impact on the degree of political participation and influence of individuals — see Fraser (1972); Frey (1971); Verba, Nie and Kim (1978); and Brady, Verba and Schlozman (1995). Hence, a given public policy in education not only has economic effects on the allocation of resources but also dynamic political consequences on the pattern of political decisions in society and the evolution of institutions. This aspect may be particularly important in many developing countries where the structure of political power is highly concentrated in the hands of a small elite. Openness, by its differential impacts on private and social incentives to accumulate human capital, may then have crucial implications for the evolution of domestic political structures.

While a full political-economy analysis of the educational response to globalisation should therefore investigate the links between openness, education and endogenous political transitions, it is convenient, as an analytical strategy, to analyse first the links between openness and public educational policies, taking as given the structure of political participation. Then, in a second step, the paper will introduce the effects of having endogenous political transitions triggered by particular educational policies.

Fixed Political Participation Structure

Consider an economy with a given structure of political participation. To simplify, suppose that the main political decision has to do with education for the poorest segment of society. In other words, assume that the liquidity constraint is binding for some part of the population. If the economy opens, the political decision will not be the same as in autarky and we want to identify this change. Clearly, it will depend on the nature of the opening (trade, capital mobility, technology transfers) and how it will affect the marginal incentives of the group in power to provide public subsidies to education. The decision will reflect the comparison between the return and the marginal cost of such a policy, as perceived by the authorities.

To be a bit more precise, consider again the Ricardo-Viner model of trade with two sectors using skilled and unskilled labour as specific factors and capital as the intersectorally mobile factor. Assume also that the group in power is the capitalist elite and consider first a situation of autarky. What are the incentives for that group to subsidise or publicly provide education? A first one, suggested in Bourguignon and Verdier (2000a), following part of the endogenous growth literature, is the idea that human capital accumulation generates externalities at the level of the aggregate economy, some or all of which can be captured by the elite. In that case, expanding the size of the educated labour force increases the return on the elite's assets beyond what market forces can provide. Another incentive emerges if skilled labour and physical capital are complements in the production process. In that case, a larger skilled labour force again increases the return on the elite's assets (Bourguignon and Verdier, 2000b).

If the elite can shift the financing cost of the educational policy on to other groups, then clearly it will have strong incentives to undertake an educational policy. If it cannot, because, for instance, these groups are too close to the limit of subsistence, it may still be in the elite's interest to pay directly part of the subsidy to education. The equilibrium educational policy will then simply reflect the trade-off between costs and benefits as perceived by the elite.

Consider first that external integration occurs through trade in goods and services. Where skilled labour and capital are scarce, the economy has a comparative advantage in the good produced with unskilled labour as a specific factor, and domestic prices become independent from domestic supply and demand conditions. When the skilled-labour-specific sector is more capital-using than the unskilled-labour-specific sector, the return to capital is less sensitive to an increase in skilled labour than under autarky. In other words, the incentives for the capitalist elite to promote education are reduced under trade openness compared with autarky[15]. The result is even stronger when one allows for international capital mobility. In that case, the return on capital is fixed by conditions ruling on international capital markets and consequently no longer depends on local factor endowments. This neutralises all incentives for the elite to promote education. Things are different for technology transfers. To the extent that they promote more complementarity between skilled labour and capital in the sector that uses skilled labour, they will clearly enhance the incentives of the capitalist elite to design policies intended to increase the skilled labour force in the economy.

In several developing economies, the political group in power may not be the capitalists but an agrarian elite owning land more complementary to unskilled than to skilled labour. How are the public choice incentives for educational policy affected in this case? A simple way to analyse this question is to amend the previous two-sector factor-specific model by introducing a third sector (agriculture, say) using land and also unskilled labour. This typical model economy has three goods ("high tech" manufactures or services, "low tech" manufactures or services and agriculture). It has four factors — skilled labour specific to high tech goods; capital, which is mobile between the two manufacturing sectors; unskilled labour, which is mobile between "low tech" manufacturing and agriculture; and land which is specific to agriculture. Suppose that the pattern of comparative advantage of the economy is to export the agricultural good and eventually the "low tech" manufacturing good and to import the "high tech" manufacturing good. Now contrast the situation where the elite comprises the capitalists to the one where the elite is agrarian.

As before, there is an incentive to promote education as this increases the return to capital, at least when skilled labour and capital are sufficiently complementary. Yet how is the return on land in the agricultural sector affected by a change of the labour force away from unskilled labour towards skilled labour? Two effects conflict. First, an increase in skilled labour attracts capital to the "high tech" sector and pushes up the return to capital. This lowers the wage rate of unskilled workers in the "low tech" sector and therefore, as unskilled labour is mobile between agriculture and "low tech" manufacturing, improves the return on land. There is a powerful countervailing force, however. By making individuals more skilled, education reduces the pool of unskilled workers available for employment in agriculture. This pushes up the unskilled wage rate and reduces the rent left to landowners. Which effect dominates will obviously depend on the technology parameters of the economy. Where unskilled labour is strongly complementary to land, the second effect is likely to dominate and the agrarian elite will not favour education. It follows, then, that the pattern of public policy towards education can be quite different depending on whether political power is in the hands of a capitalist or an agrarian elite. The former will more likely promote education than the latter.

Other political structures are of course possible but would lead to trivial decisions. For instance, if skilled workers were the decisive political agents, they would never find it in their interest to finance the education of the poorest or even to have it financed by the elite through taxes on their incomes. Indeed, skilled workers would then reduce their own incomes. The opposite would be true if unskilled workers were the decisive agents and if they had the power to impose a tax on the elite and possibly skilled workers.

Political Transitions and Openness

So far, the analysis has assumed a fixed pattern of political participation or structure of political power. This admitted no possibility for an endogenous change of political power. As discussed above, however, the political science literature widely recognises that educated individuals exert more political influence. Hence, one should expect that human capital accumulation and its associated public policies might affect endogenously the pattern of political representation in society and the evolution of political institutions. This aspect has particular interest for the determinants of political transitions and democratisation processes during economic development. It lies at the source of an important political science literature on modernisation and development (Huntington, 1968). It has also attracted some recent attention in the economics literature (Acemoglu and Robinson, 1998; Bourguignon and Verdier, 2000a, 2000b; and Robinson, 1999).

To the extent that the country's initial political situation is oligarchic and the elite anticipates, at least partially, the implications of educational policies for the future structure of political power, an obvious question comes to mind. Are the incentives for this elite to promote and subsidise the education of the poorest the same as before? That is, do the benefits it derives from the externalities emanating from education or the strong complementarity between skilled labour and capital stay the same? Or should the elite also take into account that educating too many people may lead to its losing political control? Because education may affect the profile of political participation, the elite clearly faces an additional political cost. By providing education to a large number of otherwise politically inactive individuals, it creates its own political opponents and may lose power in the future. The cost of this strategy can be a threat of expropriation by the newly educated workers, who will eventually become the pivotal agents in the political game.

Depending on the initial conditions in terms of income per capita and inequality, three basic outcomes may arise (Bourguignon and Verdier, 2000*a*). First, when the economy is poor and strongly inegalitarian, and the benefits of human capital accumulation are relatively small, the oligarchic elite does not promote education because the political cost of losing power and facing expropriation is large. The economy does not accumulate human capital; it remains stagnant and oligarchic. The second situation is just the opposite. In an initially rich, relatively egalitarian economy, with the elite's return to human capital accumulation large enough, the elite is willing to promote broad-based education. This triggers a process of democratisation and redistribution from the old elite to the newly educated classes, but it remains limited because inequality is low. Such an outcome can still be profitable to the elite if the additional growth emanating from education more than compensates for the political cost of loss of power. Finally, and maybe more interesting, there is an intermediate case. The elite solves the trade-off between its gains from education and its loss of political power by educating just the fraction of the population that allows retaining its initial political control. It promotes the emergence of a middle class large enough to reap some productivity gains from better educated workers but small enough to prevent a change of political power in the near future. This political strategy may also trigger an irreversible process of democratisation, albeit a slower one than would a widely based educational strategy.

How does openness affect the political transition? To the extent that the elite is mainly capitalist, the previous discussion suggests that trade integration will reduce the sensitivity of the elite's asset returns to changes in domestic factor endowments. This is even more true in the case of financial openness (Bourguignon and Verdier, 2000*b*). As a result, the incentives are also reduced for the elite to manipulate through educational policies the ratio of skilled to unskilled labour. The existence of a political cost in the future loss of power further accentuates this pattern. Hence, external integration, through trade and financial openness, will likely slow the process of democratisation induced by human capital accumulation, especially in the short run in a poor economy, where most individuals are close to subsistence and rely heavily on public educational policies to accumulate human capital. In the long run, however, to the extent that the poor capture some of the gains from trade owing to increased integration, external openness will be likely to increase their standard of living. They will need less public support to educate themselves. Human capital investment *cum* political participation among the poor will rely less on the control of those in power. This may help strengthen a more autonomous process of political transition towards democracy.

As before, the third option, of integration with technology transfers, may be the best to promote education and democratisation in the country. First, it may enhance the elite's incentives to broad-based educational policies, at least to the extent that skills are strongly complementary to technology transfers and that these technical innovations also increase the return to the elite's assets. Even with the political cost of losing power, this may still tilt the balance in favour of promoting education. Second, technology transfers can by themselves have political spillovers that promote democratisation directly. For example, having access to information technologies such as computers, internet and the like may increase the organisational capacity of the poor and make it more difficult for the elite to prevent or control the political transition. Given that such technology transfer cannot be opposed, this feature may even accentuate the elite's willingness to increase the size of the pie through education rather than to preserve its share of the pie. The elite may also try to choose refusing all technology transfers, but this may well be more difficult than preventing trade in goods and factor mobility.

Conclusions and Avenues for Future Research

Economic development has many facets. This paper has explored connections between two of them, openness and education. It has tried to analyse the channels through which external integration and globalisation may have an impact on the educational incentives of an initially skill-scarce developing economy. It has emphasised three main aspects. First, the effects of globalisation on domestic educational responses depend crucially on the type of international mobility implied by this process. International trade integration (goods mobility) does not have the same effects as financial integration (capital mobility), technology transfers (information mobility) or migration (labour mobility). In reality, of course, openness is often a combination of them. Technology may be embodied in import or export goods, foreign direct investment may be associated with local R&D activities and spillovers or may use the country as an exporting base, and migration can occur with remittances and better access to international credit markets for the migrants. One should therefore expect the whole effect to be a combination of what we described here for each of the "pure" facets of globalisation. Second, liquidity constraints and credit-market imperfections modify crucially the impact of external integration on the pattern of domestic human capital investment. Indeed, the effects of the "pure" dimensions of globalisation on education incentives generally reverse when individuals face important credit market imperfections in the local economy.

This second feature led to the third. Because it is quite likely that liquidity constraints are widespread in developing countries, government and public policies play a crucial role in shaping the educational effort of an economy. Hence an analysis of the impact of openness on educational responses has to take into account the effects of globalisation on the local political incentives to change public educational policies. Two aspects emerge for emphasis. First, how does openness affect the incentives of the political elite to subsidise more or less the education of poor, liquidity-constrained individuals? Second, given the special feature that education generally affects political participation positively, what impact does openness have on local political institutional changes and the associated effects on educational policies? The discussion suggests that, in general, openness makes domestic factor prices less sensitive to local factor endowments. In particular, the returns on assets owned by local elites are less affected by changes in the domestic skilled labour force. Consequently, external integration generally reduces local elites' incentives to subsidise the education of poor, unskilled individuals. A notable exception occurs when globalisation involves technology transfers strongly complementary to skilled labour. In that case, local political elites may have a strong interest in building up a large enough domestic skilled-labour force to reap the benefits of the technological improvements through enhanced returns on their productive assets. An important policy implication for international agencies is obviously to stimulate external liberalisation with intensive technology transfers[16].

On the second aspect, the impact of globalisation on local political transition, the analysis suggests for the same reasons that the immediate impact of goods and factor mobility, by reducing the elite's incentives to stimulate education, may impede in the short run the process of political liberalisation. Again, however, technology transfer and international information mobility can have a countervailing effect. In the long run, if unskilled people partly capture the gains from trade, liquidity constraints will be alleviated and more unskilled individuals will be able to fund the cost of their education, triggering an associated process of political transition. A policy implication here, for international agencies and western democracies, is to support liberalisation programmes targeted to market mechanisms ensuring that the poor are the direct beneficiaries of the gains of trade. Only under these conditions can one reasonably expect these individuals to empower themselves and stimulate a process of wider political participation.

The analysis has left aside a number of dimensions that might be worth investigating in the future. One may think about issues related to imperfections in the labour markets (segmentation, trade unions, search frictions, informational asymmetries) or in the goods market (imperfect competition, increasing returns, the public sector). The paper's assumption throughout of a small, open economy may be relaxed to allow for endogenous effects on the terms of trade. These aspects provide channels through which, directly or indirectly, globalisation will affect the local incentives and constraints to education. They await future research.

Finally, work is needed on empirical evidence in support of the various hypotheses examined. By the very nature of the issues, this evidence is difficult to gather because it can be obtained only from joint study in depth of the evolution of the structure of earnings and of the demand for schooling in the medium and long run. Such case studies are scarce, so not very much can be done for the moment. Nevertheless, the availability in several countries of repeated household surveys where both the rate of return to education and schooling behaviour can be observed during periods often extending over 15 years or more should permit making significant progress in that direction.

Notes

1. The World Bank and DELTA, Paris.

2. CERAS, DELTA, Paris and CEPR London. Correspondence: DELTA-ENS, 48 Boulevard Jourdan, 75014 Paris, France. tel: (33-1) 43.13.63.08, fax: (33-1) 43.13.63.10, e-mail: verdier@delta.ens.fr

3. For a short review of existing empirical literature on these aspects in developed countries, as well as for a critical point of view, see Atkinson (2000).

4. There is actually an important literature on trade unions and openness, which considers how the degree of labour market segmentation is affected by external liberalisation (see Gaston and Trefler, 1995; Nair-Reichert and Pomery, 1999).

5. Clearly, all these results are reversed in an economy with a comparative advantage in skilled labour. In that case trade integration increases the wage gap, induces a higher skill supply response and exacerbates the initial pattern of comparative advantage of the country.

6. It would be interesting also to consider the more realistic case where capital is an additional factor. It turns out that many of the simple results on the skilled/unskilled wage gap no longer hold. See Atkinson and Bourguignon (2000), introduction.

7. Obviously, the conclusions would be reversed if trade integration were in the first place reducing the wage gap.

8. In a small, open, unspecialised economy, factor prices depend only on international good prices and not on local factor endowments. Any factor augmenting technical change (technical change biased towards skilled or unskilled labour) therefore has no impact on these factor prices. Things are obviously different when the economy is large enough to affect international good prices. See the controversy between Leamer (1998 et 2000); and Krugman (2000).

9. Results are obviously reversed if one allows instead for migration of unskilled labour.

10. Building mainly on the insights of the endogenous growth literature in closed economies, important work has also developed dynamic trade models to explore the links between international trade, human capital accumulation and economic growth. See Lucas (1988 and1993); Rivera-Batiz and Romer (1991); Stokey (1991*a* and *b*); Young (1991); and Grossman and Helpman (1991). In these models, the

engine of growth comes from some externality generated by the process of human capital accumulation, either directly in the education sector itself or indirectly through sectoral or country-wide learning by doing. In most cases, opening induces the country to specialise according to its pattern of comparative advantage. For economies with an initial comparative advantage in unskilled labour-intensive goods, presumably without much dynamic learning capability, the educational response induced by trade liberalisation is likely to be negative.

11. All this information is taken from Bourguignon, Ferreira and Lustig (2002).

12. See also Galor and Zeira (1996) for a similar analysis endogenising the distribution of capital endowments of each generation through intergenerational bequests.

13. Note that the conclusion of the original model would not be modified if people were using some income from unskilled work to finance their education in the first period. By increasing the disposable income of the poorest, trade opening would still contribute to more investment in education. So the basic conclusion of the model may be more robust than suggested by the preceding remarks.

14. Similarly, external opening by increasing the extent of non-contractible uncertainty may push up the willingness of individuals to invest in general education rather than in industry-specific human capital, in order to promote or maintain their mobility across changing comparative advantages.

15. This is even more dramatic in the standard Hecksher-Ohlin trade model with three goods and three fully and intersectorally mobile factors (capital, skilled labour and unskilled labour). As long as all goods are produced domestically, factor prices do not depend on local factor endowments. Again this neutralises, at least at the margin, the incentives of the capitalist elite to promote public policies stimulating educational investments.

16. Reducing the stringency of TRIPs rules for poor economies, for example, may go in this direction.

Bibliography

ACEMOGLU, D. and J. ROBINSON (1998), "Why Did the West Extend the Franchise? Democracy, Inequality and Growth in Historical Perspective", mimeo, MIT, Cambridge, MA.

ATKINSON, A. (2000), "Comments on Pearson", presentation at the Conference on Poverty and Inequality in Developing Countries: A Policy Dialogue on the Effects of Globalisation, OECD Development Centre, Paris, 30 November-1 December.

ATKINSON, A. and F. BOURGUIGNON (2000), *Handbook of Income Distribution*, Elsevier, Amsterdam.

BECKER, G. (1964), *Human Capital*, 1st ed., Columbia University Press, New York, N.Y.

BERMAN, E., J. BOUND and Z. GRILICHES (1994), "Changes in the Demand for Skilled Labor within US Manufacturing: Evidence from the Annual Survey of Manufactures", *Quarterly Journal of Economics*, CIX.

BOURGUIGNON, B., C. FERREIRA and N. LUSTIG (eds.) (2002), "The Microeconomics of Income Distribution Dynamics", mimeo, World Bank, Washington, D.C.

BOURGUIGNON, F. and T. VERDIER (2000a), "Oligarchy, Democracy, Inequality and Growth", *Journal of Development Economics*, 62.

BOURGUIGNON, F. and T. VERDIER (2000b), "Openness, Education and Development: A Political Economy Perspective", *European Economic Review*, 44.

BRADY, H., S. VERBA and K.L. SCHLOZMAN (1995), "Beyond SES: A Resource Model of Political Participation", *American Political Science Review*, 89 (2).

CAMERON, S. and J. HECKMAN (1990), "The Determinants of Schooling", mimeo, University of Chicago.

CARTIGLIA, F. (1997), "Credit Constraints and Human Capital Accumulation in the Open Economy", *Journal of International Economics*, 43.

DIXIT, A. (1985), "Tax Policy in Open Economies", *in* A. AUERBACH and M. FELDSTEIN (eds.), *Handbook of Public Economics*, Vol. 1, North Holland, Amsterdam.

FEENSTRA, R. (1987), "Incentive Compatible Trade Policies", *Scandinavian Journal of Economics*, 89(3).

FEENSTRA, R. and G. HANSON (1999), "The Impact of Outsourcing and High Technology Capital on Wages: Estimates for the United States, 1979-1990", *Quarterly Journal of Economics*, X.

FINDLAY, R. and H. KIERZKOWSKI (1983), "International Trade and Human Capital: A Simple General Equilibrium Model", *Journal of Political Economy*, 91.

FRASER, J. (1972), "Political Participation and Income Level: An Exchange", *Public Choice*, Vol. 13.

FREY, B. (1971), "Why Do High Income People Participate More in Politics?", *Public Choice*, Vol. 11.

GABAIX, X. (1999), "Technical Progress Leading to Social Regress and the Losses on Trade", mimeo, Harvard University, Cambridge, MA.

GALOR, O. and J. ZEIRA (1996), "Income Distribution and International Trade", mimeo, Brown University, Providence, RI.

GASTON, N. and D. TREFLER (1995), "Union Wage Sensitivity to Trade and Protection: Theory and Evidence", *Journal of International Economics*, 39.

GROSSMAN, G. and H. HELPMAN (1991), *Innovation and Growth in the World Economy*, MIT Press, Cambridge, MA.

GUESNERIE, R. (1999), "Peut-on toujours redistribuer les gains à la spécialisation et à l'échange ? Un retour en pointillé sur Ricardo et Hecksher-Ohlin", *Revue Economique*, 3.

HILLMAN, A. (1989), *The Political Economy of Protection*, Harwood Academic Publishers.

HUNTINGTON, S. (1968), *Political Order in Changing Societies*, New Haven.

KATZ, L. and D. AUTOR (1999), "Changes in the Wage Structure and Earnings Inequality", *in* O. ASHENFELTER and D. CARD (eds), *Handbook for Labor Economics*, Vol. 3A, North Holland.

KIM, S. and Y. KIM (2000), "Growth Gains from Trade and Education", *Journal of International Economics*, 50.

KRUGMAN, P. (2000), "Technology, Trade and Factor Prices", *Journal of International Economics*, 50.

KRUGMAN, P. (1995), "Technology, Trade and Factor Prices", NBER Working Paper No. 5336.

LAWRENCE, R. and M. SLAUGHTER (1993), " Trade and US Wages: Great Sucking Sound or Small Hiccup?, *Brookings Papers on Economic Activity* No. 2.

LEAMER, E. (2000), "What's the Use of Factor Contents?", *Journal of International Economics*, 50.

LEAMER, E. (1998), "In Search of Stolper-Samuelson Linkages between International Trade and Lower Wages", *in* S. COLLINS (Ed.), *Imports, Exports and the American Worker*, The Brookings Institution, Washington, D.C.

LEAMER, E. (1994), "Trade, Wages and Revolving Door Ideas", *NBER Working Paper* No. 4716.

LEWIS, T., R. FEENSTRA and R. WARE (1989), "Eliminating Price Supports: A Political Perspective", *Journal of Public Economics*, 40(2).

LUCAS, R.E. (1993), "Making a Miracle", *Econometrica*, 61.

LUCAS, R.E. (1988), "On the Mechanics of Economic Development", *Journal of Monetary Economics*, 22.

NAIR-REICHERT, U. and J. POMERY (1999), "International R&D Rivalry and Export Market Shares of Unionised Industries: Some Evidence from the US Manufacturing Sector", *Journal of International Economics*, 49.

PSACHAROPOLOUS, G. and M. WOODHALL (1985), *Education for Development*, Oxford University Press, Oxford.

RIVERA-BATIZ, L.A. and P. ROMER (1991), "Economic Integration and Endogenous Growth", *Quarterly Journal of Economics*, 106.

ROBBINS, D. (1999), "Wage Dispersion and Trade in Colombia: An Analysis of Greater Bogota , 1976-1989", *in* C. CALLAHAN and F. GUNTER (eds): *Colombia: An Open Economy?, Contemporary Studies in Economic and Financial Analysis*, Vol. 84, Stamford, Connecticut, JAI Press.

ROBINSON, J. (1999), "When is a State Predatory?", mimeo, University of Southern California, Los Angeles, CA.

RODRIK, D. (1998), "Why do More Open Economies have Bigger Governments?" *Journal of Political Economy*, October.

RODRIK, D. (1997), *Has Globalization Gone too Far?* Institute for International Economics, Washington, D.C.

RODRIK, D. (1995), "Political Economy of Trade Policy", *in* G. GROSSMAN and K. ROGOFF (eds.), *Handbook of International Economics*, Vol. 3., Amsterdam, North Holland.

SPECTOR, D. (1999), "Is it Possible to Redistribute the Gains from Trade Using Income Taxation?", mimeo, MIT, Cambridge, MA.

STOKEY, N. (1991*a*), "The Volume and Composition of Trade between Rich and Poor Countries", *Review of Economic Studies*, 58.

STOKEY, N. (1991*b*), "Human Capital, Product Quality and Growth", *Quarterly Journal of Economics*, 106.

VERBA, S., N. NIE and J. KIM (1978), *Participation and Political Equality,* The University of Chicago Press, Chicago.

WOOD, A. (1994), "*North-South Trade, Employment and Inequality; Changing Fortunes in a Skill Driven World* ", Clarendon Press, Oxford.

YOUNG, A. (1991), "Learning by Doing and the Dynamic Effects of International Trade", *Quarterly Journal of Economics*, 106.

PART TWO

REGIONAL PAPERS: AFRICA

Globalisation, Growth and Income Inequality: The African Experience

Steve Kayizzi-Mugerwa

Since World War II, sub-Saharan Africa (SSA) has been strongly integrated into the world economy, with high trade/GDP ratios. Apart from brief spurts of growth in recent decades, however, this integration does not seem on its own to have led to sustained development. Part of the problem may lie in uneven integration into the global economy, sometimes involving capital flight and brain drain rather than resource inflows. Africa is stuck in a rut of low-value-added exports, notably agricultural commodities and minerals, which leave it exposed to international price fluctuations, attracting few technology inflows, and having few backward linkages to the rest of the economy. Yet structural impediments or initial conditions do not fully explain Africa's performance, because some "hopeless" cases have made spectacular recoveries, while more promising ones have sunk into chaos.

Growth and Reform since the 1960s

Since independence, Africa's economic performance has seen four phases. The first showed rapid growth from the mid-1960s to the early 1970s. Growing foreign debt and deteriorating performance followed, from the 1973 oil shock to the debt crisis of the early 1980s. First attempts at stabilisation and reform came in the 1980s and then more widespread market-oriented reforms in the 1990s. At independence, African economies tended to be highly dualistic, especially those which had mineral wealth, large white settler communities, or both. SSA countries had low levels of social and economic attainment as well as acute shortages of skilled personnel, aggravated by low population densities, and few could make economies of scale in provision of government services or in large private sector projects.

In the second phase, the external shocks of the 1970s exposed SSA's structural weaknesses and the rigidity of the state-dominated political and economic systems. Governments failed to cope with the situation or to preserve the gains in social-service provision following independence. Many countries borrowed heavily and introduced price controls on food and other essential commodities. This worsened economic performances and produced growing structural problems in the 1970s, culminating in a debt crisis in the early 1980s. Political and civil strife and natural disasters often exacerbated the situation.

In response, many countries, with the support of external donors, began stabilisation programmes and market-oriented reforms. Economic reforms started mostly in the mid-1980s and became fairly widespread by the early 1990s, much later than in the more developed Latin American and East Asian countries. Initial efforts tried to reduce Africa's structural vulnerability to external factors by integrating it better into the world economy through trade and capital flows, to ensure sustained growth and poverty reduction. The first generation of adjustment policies focused on macroeconomic stabilisation, emphasising exchange-rate adjustment and consolidation of government expenditure. Later reforms involved more structural matters, such as market deregulation, trade liberalisation and public-sector restructuring, including civil service retrenchment and privatisation. During the first half of the 1990s, the economic reforms of the previous decade seemed to be paying off. A number of countries showed positive growth rates and fairly low or declining inflation, but by the end of the 1990s domestic and external developments, including poor weather, continuing civil strife and the Asian crisis, led to a sharp reversal in performance.

The reforms seem to have produced little real structural transformation. In many countries, the impressive growth spurts earlier in the decade stemmed from the one-off effects of liberalising commodity marketing, which brought peasants back into formal markets buttressed by good world prices and sizeable aid inflows. There was also a "peace dividend" as South Africa came under majority rule and other trouble spots calmed down. After liberalisation, exports and imports expanded in most African countries, but diversification into manufactured exports did not happen as skilled labour was scarce because of Africa's weak educational systems. Public-sector retrenchment has actually reduced the number of modern jobs in many countries.

Poverty and Inequality

A key aspect of inequality in Africa is the huge rural-urban gap, which arises from colonial times rather than globalisation. During the long social and economic crisis, urban economies deteriorated, and in some cities pockets of poverty emerged that were worse than anything in the countryside. Poverty remains concentrated in rural areas, however, and inequality in Africa is among the highest in the world.

Trade liberalisation, by boosting export crops, actually reversed rural decline in some countries. Where crops were grown on small peasant holdings, the impact on rural welfare was clearly positive. With urban areas recovering slowly from the shock of the contracting public sector, rural-urban inequalities did not increase dramatically.

Many countries embarked on reforms in the 1980s only after the situation was already very desperate. Civil service wages were only a fraction of their levels in the 1970s, government services had deteriorated and external debt had increased. Many economies were clearly in a downward spiral. The successes and failures show some interesting features. The successes began reforms when they were on the brink of economic ruin as a result of civil war or prolonged mismanagement. They also had charismatic leaders able to trigger a sympathetic reaction from donors. The Ugandan leadership even argued successfully that, given the country's history, military expenditure was socially on a par with health and education spending. Successful governments especially had enough political clout to resist backsliding in the difficult years until the reforms bore enough fruit to compensate politically powerful losers.

Africa and the World Economy

How did the integration of Africa into the world economy fare during this period of crisis and more recent reform? The continent's trade openness declined after the first oil shock, owing largely to policy measures. It continued to do so during the 1980s crises and earlier phases of economic adjustment, as the effects on trade of poor economic growth and collapsing urban economies and infrastructure discouraged a response to policy reforms or macroeconomic measures to stimulate trade. Openness recovered a little in the 1990s owing to liberalisation, a more buoyant global economy and the overall economic revival in many African countries. Yet despite nearly 15 years of economic liberalisation, these countries have not been able to diversify their exports away from raw materials. SSA's integration into world capital markets has not changed much either. FDI inflows have been quite low, even after reforms began, compared with middle-income countries, and focused on a few successful reformers.

It is tempting to blame Africa's poor performance in the 1990s on the failure of globalisation to deliver the goods or on reforms that have not gone far enough in removing structural blocks to success. But HIV/AIDS has had a particularly devastating impact on life expectancy and decimated the working population in many countries. The disease has strained already limited social budgets, with more than half of health spending in some countries being absorbed in treating HIV/AIDS and related ailments. Civil wars and other military conflicts re-emerged in many parts of Africa in the 1990s.

Globalisation in Five Countries

Since the late 1980s, poverty in SSA, defined as those living on less than $1 per day, increased by 70 million to reach 290 million in 1998 — over 46 per cent of the population. Africa's share of the world's poor rose from just below 20 per cent to nearly a quarter. Yet Africa has substantially liberalised over the past decade and trade has recovered. Are the two processes linked or are other causes of poverty responsible?

Two pairs of countries — Côte d'Ivoire and Nigeria in West Africa, and Kenya and Uganda in East Africa — plus South Africa represent a fairly diverse set of outcomes from globalisation and liberalisation since the mid-1980s. They range from Uganda's success in restarting growth and reducing poverty to Nigeria's poor performance, with South Africa, Kenya and Côte d'Ivoire in between. Each country pair had the same type of economic structure in the early 1960s. All four pair countries had quite large and vibrant private sectors and big agricultural sectors, exporting palm oil, cocoa and coffee. South Africa's economy was much more dependent on minerals. Despite these similarities, there were major differences in land ownership and tenure patterns and, by the late 1960s, in political structures.

In both country pairs, economic reforms started only in the 1980s when external shocks and domestic problems had already seriously disrupted the economies. The extent and consistency of reform have varied substantially between countries. For much of the 1990s, Kenya had an on-off relationship with multilateral institutions. Côte d'Ivoire took a slow reform path. The oil sector dictated the pace of Nigeria's reforms, with the government unwilling to make them while oil revenues were good. Uganda followed a more consistent reform programme once it began.

The effects of liberalisation on openness have also varied. Kenya saw its level of openness fall while Uganda is working its way up from a very low base. Export concentration remains high, with most exports deriving from agriculture. As an oil exporter, Nigeria's degree of integration has moved counter-cyclically to that of its neighbours. Côte d'Ivoire, one of the more diversified SSA economies, with large quantities of manufactured exports, managed to preserve a high level of global market integration. Despite its big manufacturing sector, South Africa's market integration has been much lower than that of many SSA countries. It has increased in recent years.

During the 1960s and 1970s, *Côte d'Ivoire* had unprecedented growth, and inequality sharply increased. Inequality fell with the economic crisis of the early 1980s, then rose again with economic reforms, especially after devaluation of the CFA franc in 1994. The movements in inequality reflect the interaction of external conditions — coffee and cocoa prices — with internal inequalities in land ownership as well as the underlying economic dualism. The country had one of Africa's lowest literacy rates and life expectancies and one of its highest infant and under-five mortality rates.

Like other settler colonies, *Kenya* had a legacy of inequality of income and land ownership. Inequality increased only somewhat between 1976 and 1994, probably because the 1980s crisis had more impact on the relatively well off in urban areas, causing inequality to fall, although it rose sharply in rural areas. The difference in changes in poverty between town and country was partly due to civil strife and famine in much of rural Kenya in this period. The reforms and associated inflow of foreign money created more income-generating opportunities for the poor in towns, especially in the informal sector, than in the countryside, where only crop-producing farmers benefited directly.

Nigeria's political economy is more complex than those of other African countries. Despite its oil income, inequality there is no worse than in Côte d'Ivoire and lower than in Kenya. The inequality pattern has been similar to elsewhere, rising in the 1960s and 1970s, partly as urban, especially civil service, wages were pushed up. Inequality declined with the 1980s crisis, as oil prices and then government revenues fell, putting pressure on civil service salaries. Between 1986 and 1988, the Babangida government agreed to an IMF and World Bank structural adjustment programme but implemented it slowly and reluctantly.

The oil sector, not the government's response to pressure from multilateral institutions, was ultimately the key to economic outcomes. In the early 1990s, the world oil market was depressed and poverty in Nigeria grew by 53 per cent between 1992 and 1996. Reflecting the urban sector's increasing dependence on oil-related activities, urban poverty almost doubled, from 29.6 per cent to 57.5. Rural poverty grew less quickly but still rose by half. Because of the rent seeking and corruption that went along with oil extraction in Nigeria, the decline in social welfare and increase in inequality in the 1990s cannot be entirely blamed on structural adjustment. For example, most oil is produced in the Delta region but a poor system of rent and income sharing with the central government means that the region lags in social development behind regions with fewer resources.

Uganda has moved from the brink of economic disaster to sustained growth. Before the military took power in the early 1970s, the gini coefficient (1970) was 0.266, low compared with many African countries at the time. It was a good mirror of the economy, which rested largely on peasant farmers, some dependent on subsistence while others grew cash crops. No survey was made during the two decades of chaos that lasted until the mid-1980s. The gini coefficient for 1989 was 0.33. The fairly small change may be because, as in Kenya, the rural poor's main assets continue to be land and their own labour, which is still devoted to subsistence. By wiping out the budding middle class in the towns, forcing most heads of household to moonlight to make ends meet, the crisis had an equalising effect.

Globalisation in Uganda seems to have increased inequality very little while reducing poverty. The country has implemented economic reforms, with World Bank and IMF support, since an economic recovery programme was introduced in 1987. The reforms did not start producing growth and lower inflation until the early 1990s. The gini coefficients for 1992 and 1996 were both around 0.38. Poverty fell by 18 per cent between 1992 and 1996, with significant declines in both town and country. Only 13 per cent of the decline is thought to have resulted from changes in income distribution, with the rest due to growth in average incomes.

Uganda's reforms were successful because they raised incomes in urban and especially rural areas at the same time, and civil service wages increased from a low level. Reforms boosted incentives for production, especially in the coffee sector, through greater use of the market, removal of export taxes and related exchange-rate reforms. They resulted in higher coffee and food production in the southern parts of the country, raising incomes. At the same time, world coffee prices improved.

What the Successes Teach Us

Reintegration of sub-Saharan Africa into the global economy was a major goal of the mid-1980s reforms backed by multilateral agencies and donor countries. It was expected to reduce economic distortions and bureaucratic waste, increase FDI and technology flows and raise efficiency through greater domestic and international competition. Growth rates would rise and poverty would fall.

Three major factors have determined globalisation's impact on performance. The first is the policy response to it by governments. The erratic response by many African countries came not so much from lack of trying to implement the main elements of the Washington Consensus but because policies either could not be fully integrated, often because of missing institutions, or because they were unsuitable to local situations. The second factor in successful reform is the flow of resources from foreign donors. This depended on whether countries could negotiate with the donor community. Successful negotiations released enough goods to the population and elite groups to make further reform possible. Globalisation at its best used aid to rehabilitate social infrastructure — crucially roads in landlocked Uganda — and increase the general supply of goods and services. Reforms accompanied by inflows of funds were far less painful than the chaos the countries had gone through earlier. Donor money often preceded FDI flows.

The third factor concerns the structure of the economies, including their initial conditions and the nature of power structures. In Côte d'Ivoire, for example, reforms did not start until after the death of President Félix Houphouët-Boigny in 1993. Until then, criticism of government policy was taken as criticism of the President, the architect of earlier prosperity. Corruption came to pervade the economic system, which was only briefly disrupted by switches in military regimes. In Kenya, local capitalists could veto important parts of the programmes while in Zambia the leadership's wish for rapid globalisation clashed with the pace its supporters were willing to accept. In Nigeria, oil wealth distorted policies. Oil revenues not only boosted the government's patronage powers, but rent-seeking activities emerged around control of external trade, domestic commerce and the issuing of contracts and licences.

There are lessons to learn from the few successes. In Uganda and Ghana, globalisation worked quite well because it was seen as part of a political effort to recreate conditions for social development. This came after years of decline and civil war in Uganda and negative growth and bad governance in Ghana. Both governments had run out of easy options based on their own resources. Implementing reforms seems to have been easier in both countries because economic chaos had decimated potential opposition such as trade unions and traders, yet other previously chaotic countries have not returned to growth. The ability to improve things quickly for a large part of the population, such as farmers, was a key to success. A degree of benevolent dictatorship was at play in both Ghana and Uganda, at least during the critical initial phase of globalisation, so the quality of political leadership was decisive, but this is hard to replicate. It is also doubtful that a democratically elected government could have taken such drastic measures and stayed in power in Africa. Democracy may be desirable, but is clearly not necessary, and sometimes even an obstacle, to mobilising enough political support for sustained reform.

Globalisation cannot be entirely blamed for increased poverty and inequality in Africa in the 1990s. Social and economic afflictions and diseases, including HIV/AIDS, civil war, famine and external shocks, bear some of the blame for the low level of social achievement. Countries that are stagnant or in decline are more vulnerable to such exogenous shocks, and for many globalisation was not enough to reverse the negative social trends. In the success stories, such as Ghana, Uganda and Mozambique, globalisation revived investment and growth, helping governments to start tackling poverty.

It is hard to say which way African economies would have gone in the absence of globalisation. That many countries applied the standard model of it without success is sobering. Is the model flawed or is its implementation? In the few successful cases, strong political leadership was clearly crucial early on, with top leadership directly involved in the debate. There also was willingness, perhaps because policy making capacity had been decimated during the chaos of the previous decades, to rehabilitate and reform government institutions. The successful countries also benefited from a kind of "sympathy premium" from donor agencies, which did not impose their conditions too strictly.

The Political Economy of Globalisation, Poverty and Inequality in Sub-Saharan Africa

Yvonne M. Tsikata

Implementation of globalisation reforms in Africa has been uneven and the policy response generally inadequate. Except in Mauritius, compensation has not been systematically offered, reflecting weak capacity and politicisation of the process, so globalisation has largely failed to achieve sustainable pro-poor growth. Some countries have liberalised trade rapidly and comprehensively (Ghana and Zambia), and some in a sustained but gradual manner (Mauritius and Uganda), while others failed to open up seriously until quite recently, often reversing policies along the way (Kenya, Nigeria and Senegal). This suggests that it is possible to liberalise and reduce poverty and inequality (Ghana and Uganda) but that greater emphasis on compensation (Mauritius) is more sustainable.

Country variations were mostly due to political and institutional differences, state capacity and external factors. Economic crisis and political change gave some non-democracies a mandate to liberalise in the short run (Ghana and Uganda), but crisis was neither necessary (Mauritius) nor sufficient for liberalisation to occur. It did insulate regimes and gave them the political space to act. In the long run, however, a political system with accountability and coalition building (as in Mauritius) seems to make balancing the costs and benefits of globalisation easier and is more sustainable than crisis-driven reforms. State capacity allows a country independently to design and implement complementary policies and, with leadership, determines how skilfully a regime can negotiate and build consensus around a response to globalisation.

Mauritius successfully globalised by finding the right balance between fostering efficiency through competition and building the capacity of the state and economic actors to participate in globalisation. It shows that supply-side policies in credit, infrastructure, skill development and technological support are critical for successfully adjusting to global competition. Simple, well-designed compensatory programmes are just as important and allow the government to gain respect by fulfilling the social contract. Supply-side and compensatory policies validate and empower losers, making for less resistance to reforms. Mauritius shows the benefit of electoral accountability, which forces coalition building and encourages leaders to ensure broad-based, equitable growth. This feeds back through the electoral process as support for reform, creating a virtuous circle. Ghana and Uganda show that while non-democracies can successfully liberalise, the transition to multiparty democracy or pressures for it can either derail liberalisation or become a distraction. Lack of accountability and openness can also make it hard to build coalitions for liberalisation even among the winners.

Ghana, Uganda and Zambia show that clear breaks with the past can be important in sustaining reforms. Interest groups have less influence on the path and pace of liberalisation, and policy reversal is rare. Where political regimes are "business as usual" despite changes in leadership, interest groups are more influential in dictating the process of liberalisation. Ghana and Uganda also show that supporting agriculture is important to how pro-poor the response to globalisation is. Nigeria, Zambia and other mineral-rich countries confirm that skewed asset distributions create unequal distribution of political power, leading to poor policy and unsustainable reform.

How Africa Globalised

Before globalisation, Africa's integration into the world economy was rather contradictory. In some ways it was quite high even in the early 1970s. Trade to GDP ratios were among the highest in the world owing to the important role of raw material exports. Labour flows were substantial owing to the brain drain. Yet flows of private capital were small, most countries had major policy barriers to all kinds of trade and capital flows, and much of the trade that did occur was through state or monopoly bodies.

Globalisation began later in Africa than elsewhere and has been less advanced. Trade liberalisation has been quite varied, with "strong" (Ghana, Uganda and Zambia), "weak" (Nigeria and Zimbabwe) and "intermediate" (Côte d'Ivoire, Kenya, Mauritius, Senegal, South Africa and Tanzania) liberalisers. Capital account liberalisation occurred in fewer countries and is less advanced, and capital flows are still concentrated in a few countries. So Africa has actually become more marginalised and less integrated in the world economy over the past two decades relative to other regions. A few countries have changed substantially (non-traditional exports have grown rapidly in Ghana and Uganda).

Globalisation's impact on poverty is not determined only by the degree of liberalisation, but also by how countries have responded with supply-side and compensatory policies. The region's performance has been slow and inadequate. Only a few countries have invested in education — the key to benefiting from globalisation — while primary school enrolment even fell in many countries. Most introduced compensatory measures (overwhelmingly public works programmes) but these measures seem to have compensated only direct losers. The responses have not been strategically planned and have been too often reactive or politically driven and therefore poorly targeted, including badly targeted and often regressive spending. Mauritius is the only country that systematically and successfully implemented supply-side policies to meet globalisation's challenges. Ghana and Zimbabwe had pockets of success but could not come up with coherent strategies. Ranking all the countries for the quality of their macroeconomic, supply-side and liberalisation policies, Mauritius came first, Ghana and Uganda second, Tanzania third, South Africa, Zambia and Zimbabwe fourth and Côte d'Ivoire, Nigeria and Senegal last. Good policy means that the policies were initiated, implemented and sustained over the medium term, with appropriate speed and sequencing.

Great diversity in inequality might be expected in view of the wide diversity of liberalisation and offsetting measures in the region. It is hard to get a clear picture of income inequality and poverty trends because sampling dates are infrequent and vary across countries, with little data before the mid-1980s. Only two countries (Ghana and Mauritius) come out as clearly "good performers" in terms of inequality. Assessment of trends in Côte d'Ivoire, Tanzania and Uganda depends on the choice of starting date. In Nigeria, inequality has clearly worsened. In most other countries, except Mauritius, inequality declined somewhat. The poverty picture is even more mixed. It increased substantially (measured by the headcount ratio) in Nigeria and Zimbabwe and decreased in Uganda and Ghana. Ghana and Mauritius performed well on both counts, with progress on one or the other in Tanzania and Uganda. Elsewhere, both poverty and inequality were stable or increased.

If the rankings are compared in terms of performance in policy and inequality, the top three performers in growth, poverty reduction and inequality (Ghana, Mauritius and Uganda) also lead the policy ranking. This suggests that supply-side and compensatory policies are necessary but not sufficient to generate pro-poor growth (Zimbabwe failed to improve despite good supply policy). Zambia and South Africa show that liberalisation without supporting policies gives unsatisfactory distribution results and, in Zambia, makes liberalisation unsustainable.

Economic growth is needed to sustain commitment to reform, so favourable external conditions (commodity prices) are important in determining which policies are chosen and whether they are sustained. Three other important factors are the nature of political institutions (regime, accountability and ideology), state capacity and external resources. Consensus is much harder to achieve in countries with deep distributional conflicts based on historically based racial, tribal and other divisions (South Africa, Zimbabwe and Nigeria). Ideology also plays a role in the commitment by leaders in Uganda and Zimbabwe to redistributive policies, as compared with a fairly *laissez-faire* approach in Zambia. Political space is not sufficient to generate good policy, because adequate state capacity is required to design and implement it. Many countries introduced a range of programmes, but weak administrative capacity meant poor implementation. Mauritius (with the best human capital) had the most complex safety nets.

Policy Lessons

What are the lessons for policy? First, liberalisation is likely to be more sustainable when it generates good outcomes or can compensate losers. Sustainable liberalisation and good outcomes in turn require complementary policies and institutions. In the short run, countries may be able to use liberalisation to reduce poverty without investing heavily in complementary measures. They can tap into unused capacity in manufacturing (Ghana) and revitalise depressed export or food-crop sectors (Ghana and Uganda) to create employment and reduce poverty. This often happens when building on activities that do not require investment in infrastructure, such as the revival of coffee in Uganda, and when commodity prices are favourable.

In the medium term, however, the ability of any growth recovery to provide sustained benefits to the poor depends on complementary policies. Providing credit, developing skilled managers and technicians, labour market reforms, strengthening the technological base in rural and urban areas, providing inputs to agriculture and targeted interventions to reduce the vulnerability of the poor seem the most important. Even for natural resource-based revivals, complementary infrastructure is often necessary (feeder roads for cocoa, credit for farmers and mine upgrading in Ghana). Complementary policies can keep even non-targeted winners doing well. In Ghana, petty traders and the informal sector in rural and urban areas benefited from the increased incomes and ready availability of land and credit under the PAMSCAD safety net. In South Africa, however, while gradual trade liberalisation may have partly stemmed job losses, failure to address labour market issues (or to do so only belatedly) and slowness in upgrading skills reduced competitiveness exactly when it needed to be enhanced. Other labour market policies, such as government reluctance to introduce different wages for young people and in depressed areas, probably hurt the poor.

Second, strengthening complementary policies means boosting state capacity (both individuals and institutions), especially as the kinds of policies needed to respond to globalisation, such as labour market policies, are more complex, requiring more negotiation and consensus-building than macroeconomic stabilisation. Civil service reforms that encompass professionalism, merit-based service and decent pay are a step in the right direction. Strengthening the ability to generate resources through taxes is also important to help pay for potential compensation, reduce aid dependency and gain greater autonomy over policy. Boosting the capacity of non-government agencies and individuals who can advise policy makers and increase a government's accountability is critical too.

Third, the pace and sequencing of reforms are critical determinants of the impact of globalisation on the poor. A balance has to be found between fostering efficiency through competitive pressures and building capabilities. A more gradual pace allows establishment of institutions and policies to support the restructuring of existing firms and emergence of new ones, new products and new crops. In Zambia, over-rapid trade liberalisation and tight monetary policy led to job losses and decimation of

56

industry. Incorrect sequencing of monetary and liberalisation reforms led to financial problems for farmers and, concerning the capital account and monetary policy, led to a kwacha appreciation at odds with the goals of the liberalisation package. South Africa's liberalisation of the capital account, however, was done cautiously, with clear advance signals given and appropriate supporting institutions established first. In Mauritius, gradual liberalisation allowed for a decline in sugar's importance while social institutions and EPZs allowed emergence of new winners and opportunities.

Fourth, establishing a suitable political and institutional framework to guide the interrelated policies of liberalisation, social policies and other complementary reforms is crucial. Liberalisation may occur when reformers are either insulated from opposing interests in non-democratic governments (pre-1992 Ghana and Uganda) or when new interests emerge to support reform (Mauritius), which is more attractive and desirable for the long-term political sustainability of the reforms. An electoral system that forces leaders to look beyond a narrow set of interests, as in Mauritius, is the way to build popular support for liberalisation. Building coalitions for reforms, even in countries that experience growth and poverty reduction, has been notoriously hard. Reasons include the classic free-rider problem and difficulties of collective action, fragmented organisations (farmers, business) that contain both winners and losers, cross-cutting rather than organisational interests and sometimes political ambivalence towards the regime despite economic gains. External support for "passive" winners may sometimes help, but this can backfire.

The system's ability to allow emergence of demand-based projects to redress the costs of adjustment, distribute benefits from growth, dialogue with the private sector and encourage citizen participation in political and policy processes are all part of establishing the suitable political framework. Establishing an internally consistent democratic social contract calls for leadership with an economic and social vision, political accountability, broadened dialogue with the population and coalition building. Societal consensus helps but is not necessary. Strengthened capacity of civic organisations (particularly those not usually having a voice) and the media, and continued support by donors for multi-party democracy, are critical to enhancing the policy dialogue and debate.

Fifth, improved agricultural performance is often a major component of pro-poor responses to globalisation in Africa because it ensures that growth is labour intensive, as in Ghana, Uganda and early Zimbabwe. This works for most countries except the very urbanised and industrialised. Africa has nowhere near experienced a "green revolution", so boosting agricultural productivity and output through adequate credit, inputs and technological improvements is a priority.

Finally, external support (both ideas and finance) can be important in offsetting some costs associated with globalisation or offering new directions. Aid can offset terms-of-trade losses and fund social safety nets and infrastructural improvements (Ghana and Uganda). Ideas can also come from other countries — Ghana's earlier adjustment effort influenced the Ugandans who decided on a more gradual approach. Chinese (and also French) connections taught Mauritius many things.

Rapporteur's Report on Sub-Saharan Africa Regional Session

Daniel Cohen, Rapporteur for the Africa Regional Breakout Session

We had a very exciting discussion on Africa. People spoke very frankly and openly, as the diplomats say. The debate on globalisation became a global debate, as speakers took a very broad view of things, although of course there was a great deal of talk about the fluctuation of the terms of trade, commodity prices and the like. Topics included a number of domestic reforms not directly linked to external integration — industrial relations, for example, and the privatisation of public services and public utilities, telephones, restructuring the public service and the role played by financial adjustment programmes put in place by the World Bank and the IMF. Globalisation is viewed in a number of countries as the interrelation of all these factors, and it is very difficult to delineate causes and effects. Globalisation is not just about trade or the liberalisation of financial services. It involves everything from the reform of the public sector to the privatisation of public utilities.

Most of the speakers said that in Africa in particular, and this applies to other countries as well, inequalities are important of course, but they are so poorly measured that we have to consider them as indicators of the various ills that these countries are experiencing. In a period of crisis inequalities are less important quite simply because the most vulnerable people are no longer accounted for in the statistics. Constant interactions between the formal and the informal sectors — the latter means the people who are the most vulnerable — tend to disappear from the formal sector and no longer appear in the statistics. For example, when cocoa prices went down in Côte d'Ivoire most of the migrant workers went back home and so they were no longer included in the statistics on inequality. They simply weren't taken into account. If you look at statistics on inequalities you can see a reduction towards the end of the 1990s, whereas the number of poor people increased. That said, Africa has the highest incidence of poverty. Between 1997 and 1999 the number of poor there increased tremendously — by 70 million — and that does not appear in statistics on inequalities.

The speakers were very severe when discussing globalisation. In the first half of the discussion people said that globalisation was a new form of imperialism, a necessary evil that benefits the major corporations but not necessarily the general population. In the second half of the debate, a number of other factors were mentioned that explained poverty in Africa apart from globalisation. A key distinction emerged between endogenous and exogenous globalisation. Exogenous globalisation has existed for a long time in most African countries and it simply means an extreme dependence on commodities and raw materials, and vulnerability to fluctuations of the terms of trade. Many examples given showed how growth strategies were not sustained because of fluctuation of the terms of trade for cocoa and coffee, for example. The effects go far beyond a loss of revenues for those concerned. Consider the demographic effects. In African countries, people have more children to help them work on their coffee plantations. When there is a problem with the terms of trade the whole sector deteriorates. All these children remain, with no alternatives. There is insufficient education, so they simply stay home. This creates a vicious circle and the effects are catastrophic. Sao Tomé et Principe was cited as another example of a country undertaking serious reforms that was stopped in its tracks by exogenous globalisation, dependence on something over which it had no control.

The role of women was raised a number of times, because in most cases it's women more than men who have jobs in the cities. In most cases women suffer from deterioration in the terms of trade and bear the brunt of the inequalities.

Endogenous globalisation, by contrast, involves increased industrialisation. Countries accept it voluntarily. It decreases inequalities and is actually desired. So globalisation is rather ambiguous. It creates opportunities, but it also creates risks because of increased dependence. One must be extremely cautious in trying to draw lessons. In Uganda, for example, dependence leads to fragility. Imports there increased threefold, whereas exports only doubled. That creates a situation of financial dependence on other countries. It could reverse fast in a future crisis and be very destabilising and immiserising. Most globalisation has been brought in from outside; it is exogenous globalisation and lacks the necessary strong accompanying role of government.

Discussion of reform of the state led to a number of criticisms levelled at the World Bank and the IMF. It was said that the two institutions have a rather naïve view of what globalisation involves and perhaps they underestimate the necessary role of government in accompanying this process. When they monitor financial adjustment and financial and economic liberalisation, what they do in fact is replace the government and the public debate that should have taken place. There should be a democratic, open, public debate, but they short-circuit it and there is no appropriate public response. Mauritius serves as a counter-example, because to a certain extent it could engage a public debate on the policies necessary to accompany its economic opening strategy. The measures advocated by the Fund and Bank are not sufficient. If growth and development are to succeed in Africa, public debate on the necessary accompanying measures is all the more necessary now. We need ownership. It is not sufficient to have exogenous globalisation, and nothing can replace an internal debate.

PART THREE

REGIONAL PAPERS: LATIN AMERICA

Distribution and Growth in Latin America in an Era of Structural Reform: The Impact of Globalisation

Samuel A. Morley

Globalisation in Latin America since the early 1980s has involved a shift from import substitution to export promotion as part of structural adjustment programmes in response to the 1982 debt crisis. Current and capital account liberalisation and extensive domestic reforms were the basis of an export-led growth strategy to align domestic with world prices and increase the market's role in allocating resources and investment to improve efficiency and drive down costs. This was supposed to increase competitiveness, exports and growth.

The region has long had the world's most unequally distributed income, due to highly unequal distribution of farmland, government development and education policies and demography. This produced rapid growth in unskilled labour and increased demand for university-trained workers, widening the earnings gap. Import substitution, which had produced high growth and high inequality, also involved more and more structural imbalances, greater foreign borrowing and eventually a debt crisis. Economic reforms were then introduced and inequality increased further during the economic stagnation of the "lost decade" of the 1980s. At the start of the 1990s, hope emerged that reforms would bring recovery and growth, but unfortunately neither has occurred. Why has that happened and how much do the structural reforms have to do with it?

Determinants of Income Distribution

Inequality is a serious problem in Latin America. Only three of the countries studied had low or declining inequality and adequate growth. In the others — containing over 90 per cent of the region's population — inequality stayed stubbornly high or had risen significantly in recent years, or the countries were in serious recession.

Why is inequality so high? One of its components is the distribution of earnings. The interaction between supply and demand for the factors of production and the distribution of factor ownership determine it initially. The region's persistently high inequality arises largely from an unequal distribution of the four key productive assets — land, capital and skilled and unskilled labour. All but unskilled labour have unequal distributions compared with industrialised countries and other developing areas. Two of them, skilled labour and capital, are scarce, which means their rates of return are high. This has been exacerbated by the skill- and capital-intensive growth strategy, which has boosted profit rates and the return to education.

Latin America has always had the world's most unequal land distribution, with the four most unequal countries and seven others in the top 16. Land reform has been mostly unsuccessful because it did not affect very many landholdings or significantly equalise ownership. Unskilled rural labour is paid very little in countries with very unequal land distribution. Rather than confronting the powerful landed oligarchs, Latin America's rural poor escape by migrating to the cities, which avoids violent confrontation but drives down the wage of the urban unskilled.

To make things worse, the population growth rate rose between 1950 and 1980 as death rates fell with better health care. This greatly increased the size of younger age groups, which had to be educated or absorbed into the labour force. The education system did not expand enough to cope, so most entered the job market with meagre education, swelling the supply of unskilled labour. Without access to land and other productive inputs, they drove down rural wages and then flooded into the cities, driving down unskilled wages there too. At the same time, most countries in the region developed with import substitution, involving rapid growth in demand for and returns to skilled labour and capital. This led to a rise in informalisation, stagnation in real wages for the unskilled and a bigger wage gap. An over-supply of poorly educated workers has been created that will have regressive effects on income inequality until the demographic transition comes to an end, further challenging government efforts to reduce inequality. Faster and more labour-intensive growth and investment in secondary education are needed.

Human Capital and Education

Education is a key to the distribution puzzle. Latin America has a very unequal distribution of education or human capital and the highest skill differentials in the world. Education and experience are the major determinants of where a person is to be found in the income distribution picture. Another puzzle is the region's persistently high education wage differentials, which cannot be explained by scarcity of university graduates. Latin America has a bigger proportion of university graduates than Asia but higher returns to university education. The number of these graduates in Latin America has grown rapidly since 1970, yet skill differentials have widened. This is a key reason why inequality has not declined in the region. Why has greater supply not reduced education differentials and rates of return to university education?

The white-collar wage differential in Latin America in 1982 was double that of developed countries and 50 per cent higher than in the four Asian tigers. Since then, it has fallen everywhere but in Latin America, despite the region's growing proportion of college and high school graduates. It has even risen sharply there since 1988. Latin America's large proportion of university graduates contrasts with the small number of people with high school education. Most countries have universalised primary education, sharply reducing the percentage of the labour force without any education. Many children still do not go beyond primary school, so much of this progress has been offset by an increase in those with no more than primary education. In Asia, the proportion of secondary and university graduates nearly doubled between 1970 and 1985, but in Latin America, university graduates expanded twice as fast as those finishing secondary school. Asia universalised secondary education while Latin America chose to expand university coverage.

Because Latin America has expanded the supply of university graduates faster than Asia, its rising relative wages or returns to university education cannot be attributed to failure to expand supply. Its focus on university education has also increased the variance in ownership of human capital, or educational inequality. When a country upgrades education, this inequality will increase as the education of the young improves relative to older age groups. That trend reverses as older people retire and are replaced by better and more equally educated younger people. Latin America's educational strategy has delayed this turning point. Not only is educational inequality still increasing, it is doing so faster than expected.

Upgrading the labour force by investing in education is a key part of any government's social policy. Yet it takes a long time to affect earnings distribution significantly (when the newly educated join the labour force) partly because it takes a long time to produce a well-educated worker and partly because each entering cohort is small relative to the entire labour force. Thus it is impossible to alter quickly the variance of education or the educational profile of the workforce, so a real change in earnings inequality has to come from changes in the rate of return to education — the wage differential.

Unfortunately, wage differentials are moving in favour of the more educated. The rise in the university group contribution to overall inequality is so great that it completely offsets favourable trends among the rest of the population and is responsible for all the increase in inequality. More demand for university skills outstripped even the growing supply, a striking result of increasingly skill-intensive growth in the 1990s. Growth in the new economic model strongly favoured the few in the labour force with university education. We do not know whether this was the result of opening up the economy, of an increase in the market power of university graduates or of changes in technology.

Growth and Inequality

Growth is the most important way the distribution of earnings changes. It is an unbalancing process that spreads unevenly across economies, starting in a particular sector or region and trickling down to the rest of the economy through linkages.

Some Latin American economies have weak linkages, such as backward regions or indigenous populations only marginally connected to modern dynamic sectors. They contain much of the population, so their income levels will have a noticeable effect on inequality. Growth in these conditions tends to be inequitable. Inequality is likely to be lower the smaller and more homogenous the economy.

Just as important is a country's growth strategy. If substantial growth comes from sectors that use a lot of unskilled labour, such as construction or agriculture, it will be equalising, as it will if the leading sectors are in backward regions. If the leading sector is skilled-labour intensive or in mineral extraction — which does not employ many people directly and has weak links with the rest of the economy — growth will very probably increase the skill differential and worsen inequality. The government can play a big role in determining the size of the linkage or spread effect of growth. It can generate much demand for the unskilled through construction and spend money on backward regions. So even if the basic growth comes from mineral extraction or skill-intensive exports, the government can use the tax revenues they generate to fund construction projects or other activities such as basic health care, education or direct transfers that will help the poor and raise the demand for unskilled labour.

Empirically there seems to be a robust and significant relationship between growth and the distribution of income, but it is not unidirectional. Growth will increase inequality in low-income countries until they reach the income level of Colombia or Costa Rica, after which it will fall. At the same time it appears that growth is less equitable in the region than it used to be, since it is more skill-intensive. It has widened wage differentials and boosted the rate of return to education.

The Effects of Structural Reform

Latin America has undergone massive structural reform in recent years. Reform began in the Southern Cone in the 1970s, spread through the rest of the region after 1985, usually as part of structural adjustment packages, and boosted the role of the market in resource allocation. Trade reforms removed tariff protection from domestic production and financial reforms and privatisation reduced government influence over resource allocation. Balance of payments reforms integrated foreign and domestic capital markets and reduced the government's ability to control capital movements, while labour-market reform increased flexibility, reducing labour's ability to defend itself against market-driven demand fluctuations and wage reductions.

How have these changes affected equity? A key feature of neo-liberal reforms in Latin America has been reduced tariffs and greater reliance on exports. This should have helped unskilled labour, which is abundant in the region, but instead wage differentials are growing in favour of skilled labour in most countries despite increasing supply.

What is the effect of liberalising the capital account? This integrates local and international capital markets more closely, bringing local interest and profit rates closer to those in the rest of the world. If foreign investors have been put off because of restrictions on capital flows and profit repatriation, reforms should induce a foreign capital inflow. Wage/profit ratios should rise because of the rise in the capital/labour ratio. That is progressive, but if capital and skilled labour are complementary, the skill differential will rise, which is regressive.

If foreign investors are free to move from one country to another, governments will find it far more difficult to tax capital or force businesses to shoulder more of the cost of infrastructure or labour regulation. They also will be obliged to compete in costly ways to attract foreign capital — the so-called "race to the bottom". Both government and labour will be forced to induce domestic entrepreneurs to leave their money invested locally. This is one reason there has been a shift away from taxation of corporate profits and a big reduction in the top income tax rate in Latin America in recent years.

Domestically, the main components of reform were in finance, taxation and privatisation. Financial reforms eliminated controls on interest rates, cut compulsory reserve requirements of banks and reduced the use of directed or subsidised credit. The direct effect on inequality has probably been small. Tax reform has usually comprised a value-added tax (VAT) and cuts in marginal tax rates. During the 1970s and 1980s, VAT was introduced in all 17 countries. Enforcement is easier than with an income-tax system. This and cuts in top income tax rates shifted away from taxation of income (the wealthy) towards taxation of consumption, which hurts poorer people. The overall effect is regressive.

The effect of privatisation on distribution depended on the sale price, the price of services and labour demand. If the assets of state-owned enterprises (SOEs) were sold for less than their market value, the buyers were in effect receiving a gift from taxpayers. Many public utilities subsidised their customers by setting prices below cost. The distributional impact depended on the price of these services to the public after privatisation, which usually meant eliminating the subsidy. Labour demand and employment were also affected. Labour productivity in the typical SOE was low because, for political reasons, many governments were more interested in using these enterprises to create high-wage jobs than to provide good, cheap service. Privatisation mostly hurt the urban middle class, the main users of subsidised SOE services and the main employees of such state-owned firms.

Regression analysis suggests that the economic reforms have had an overall regressive effect on the distribution but it is small and only marginally significant compared with factors such as growth, inflation and changes in education structure. Trade reform is regressive but largely insignificant. Tax reform is clearly regressive and opening up the capital account clearly progressive.

How to Find Sustainable and Rapid Growth

Despite the attention to the growth-distribution relationship, the more serious question in Latin America now is the growth rate itself, which fell sharply in the late 1990s. Before the Tequila Crisis in 1995, growth was much higher than in the 1980s and things were expected to get even better because of the recently implemented reforms. This did not happen. An export slowdown created a big part of the problem. The export-promotion model is not working very well, particularly in South America. At first it seemed rather successful, and most countries' exports provided the biggest source of demand growth in the first half of the 1990s. Since 1995, exports from almost every country in South America have substantially declined, forcing most economies to slow down by reducing imports and conserving foreign exchange. In contrast, every country in Central America increased its exports. This difference is mostly due to market conditions. South American exports go mainly to Asia and Europe, where there has been slow growth, while those from Central America and the Caribbean go to the United States, which had an extended boom. Latin America is also losing market share because its exports are growing too slowly.

Exports by South America have not provided the strong growth needed for very rapid income growth. The region has found that export-led growth can easily become an export-led decline when external markets contract significantly. Latin America may also be specialising in the wrong products or the wrong countries, or perhaps exporters have failed to modernise and cut costs to compete better against other developing countries.

What Should Be Done?

The reappearance of the growth problem and insensitivity of the distribution to feasible policies implies that the main policy focus in the region ought to be how to increase growth rather than how to improve the distribution. Recent experience suggests, however, that achieving an adequate and sustainable growth rate will be harder now. Globalisation has many advantages but also many tough challenges for economic managers. The most important target a government can have is to achieve the highest and most stable growth rate possible. It must not rely excessively on borrowing since that will affect future growth. High but unstable growth rates do as much harm as good, and high rates that trigger significant inflation will have a regressive effect. Stable, rapid growth is a necessary, although not sufficient, condition for reducing poverty and unemployment and increasing wages for the least qualified.

A complementary goal is to absorb as much unskilled labour as possible without unduly sacrificing the overall growth rate. Latin America's basic distribution problem lies in reducing the supply of such labour and increasing the demand for it. A growth strategy that creates a lot of jobs for unskilled labour takes care of demand while investment in education will help reduce supply. Construction and agriculture, as big users of unskilled labour, should play a key part in the equitable growth strategy, which should also favour production of traded goods, because they too use a lot of unskilled labour.

Backward regions should also be a priority. Growth is almost always sparked by something that happens in a sector or region, but the more heterogeneous and fragmented an economy or country is, the less such events will affect other sectors or regions. Governments should try to increase the spread or linkage effects of growth, for example by improving transport and communications in backward regions and making special efforts to upgrade worker training and education there.

A major part of Latin America's distribution problem comes from the large supply of unskilled labour relative to the demand for it, a result of many years of high population growth and inadequate education. Until that surplus is eliminated, wage differentials are unlikely to narrow and not much progress will be made on equity. Latin America is hostage to past policy failures that will take a long time to correct. Labour-intensive growth will help, but more important in the long run is an education strategy with the objective of providing everyone entering the labour market with at least secondary education. This will, over a few years, significantly reduce the growth of unskilled labour and boost that of skilled labour. Skill differentials will then start narrowing and equity will improve.

Education should also be a key part of equity-increasing growth strategy because raising the level of young people's education reduces a colossal waste of human potential. How many would-be entrepreneurs or scientists are working in agriculture or the informal sector just because they never got enough education to unlock that potential? Human capital is more and more vital for growth, so education is as important as investing in machinery. Universalising education also makes sense because, rich or poor, parents are concerned about their children's future. If the poor see that the state provides a good secondary school education, they are more likely to accept an unequal distribution of their own income. They will see that inter-generational inequality is falling, even if the statistics do not show it. Inter-generational mobility matters and education is the key to increasing it.

Significant progress has been made in recent years in reducing poverty and expanding education coverage in younger age-groups, but the distribution indexes do not reflect that. Latin America needs to keep going down the road of faster, more labour-intensive growth and broadening the coverage of secondary education. That will lower poverty levels and raise real wages for the unskilled and eventually produce declining inequality indexes.

Where Does Inequality Come From?
Ideas and Implications for Latin America

James A. Robinson

Western European and East Asian countries have much less inequality than today's Latin America. Yet in the past, Western Europe had just as much. The key factor in egalitarian trends in Europe over the past century has been democratisation, especially of political institutions, leading to political parties that pressed for mass education and redistribution of income through the tax system. This created societies with much more upward mobility and sharply reduced asset and income inequality.

Distribution of income in a society is said to depend on the distribution of income-generating assets or factors of production — who owns the land and capital and how human capital is distributed in the labour force — and on the returns to these assets. If asset distribution were exogenous, preferences and technology would determine the distribution of income (inequality differences). Countries can have very different asset distributions despite identical preferences and technology, however, because initial conditions and historical circumstances come into play. Redistribution of assets, such as land or educational reforms, may have permanent effects on subsequent inequality. Land is not the only key asset determining income distribution. Human capital is now probably even more important.

In Latin America, asset ownership does not evolve naturally to any level. It is highly skewed because of unequal distribution of land and education, reflecting history, institutions and political conditions. However these assets are distributed, institutions and government policies determine the rates of return they earn, not just preferences and technology.

How Globalisation Works

Globalisation affects inequality when the distribution of assets is fixed and it can change the rates of return on different assets under an unchanged set of institutions and policies. It may also alter the distribution of assets by, say, massively increasing

71

incentives to expropriate the assets of others. The most obvious example of the first effect is when a country specialises on the basis of comparative advantage. As Latin America joined the world economy in the late 19th century, it specialised in producing commodity exports to the industrial world, increasing the rate of return to the abundant factor, land. The second big effect of globalisation was that the increase in the rate of return on land increased the incentives to own it. Because property rights are endogenous, this led to big changes in land distribution that depended crucially on differences in political power structures.

Yet political and institutional equilibrium is itself influenced by globalisation, which can affect the political and bargaining power of domestic actors, who in turn can use globalisation to increase their power. Globalisation is not an exogenous force influencing a society as if it were rainfall. The decision to integrate with or separate from world markets is endogenous and may be part of a new political equilibrium with important consequences for inequality. While international factors such as the impact of GATT (now the WTO) are largely exogenous to developing countries, it was no coincidence that the military regimes in Chile (after 1973) and Argentina (after 1976) were the first Latin American countries to embrace globalisation. Trade liberalisation, which weakened their domestic opponents, such as trade unions powerful in the import substitution sector, was politically important and increased the power of these regimes.

Globalisation may change relative prices and induce changes in the distribution of assets. If it increases inequality in this way, it may simultaneously alter the political equilibrium and stop the state compensating for these effects. The main criticism of globalisation is that it bundles such forces together in a unique way that both increases inequality and removes the state's ability to compensate for it. Nevertheless, globalisation can also go hand in hand with dramatically falling inequality. What really determines its effect on inequality is a country's political equilibrium, which seems largely governed by forces other than globalisation. Its impact depends on how it is handled by domestic institutions. It does not by itself prevent governments from responding.

Inequality in Latin America

Differences in inequality are huge in Latin America and very high compared with OECD or Asian countries. These differences and their change over time come from differences in the underlying distribution or rates of return on assets and their determinants (technology, preferences and institutions) that map the distribution of assets into a distribution of income. Land is much more unequally distributed in Latin America than in Western Europe, North America or East Asia. Latin American countries have been catching up in literacy and primary enrolment but are still far behind in other ways, such as secondary enrolment, suggesting that human capital is more unequally distributed in Latin America than in Europe or North America. Specialising in mineral or agricultural exports seems to increase inequality by reducing the incentive to accumulate human capital, except where agricultural land ownership is not highly concentrated.

What causes the differences in labour market institutions or the educational system that produce big differences in inequality? The strength of the egalitarian impulse induced by democratisation seems to depend on whether a socialist party emerged and won power. Differences in the party system appear to be an important part of persistent inequality in Latin America and are closely related to the political institutions and the history of political development. Globalisation involves either rising or falling inequality, but the actual distribution of assets and income depends on other factors, such as institutions and politics. There is no evidence that globalisation is significantly connected to them. Cross-country differences in income inequality in Latin America seem related to inequality in land distribution and educational attainment. Asset and thus income distribution is greatly affected by the presence or absence of democracy.

Democracy and Inequality

Argentina's pattern of inequality matches its political history — falling during democratic periods and rising under dictatorships. Inequality fell rapidly during the 1920s, rose at the end of the authoritarian 1930s and fell dramatically under Perón's more populist administration. After his overthrow in 1955, it rose rapidly, stayed mostly unchanged during the 1960s and fell again during the second Peronist administration from 1973 to 1976. After the 1976 coup, it rose sharply, although it increased during the 1990s, the first instance of rising inequality in Argentina during democracy. In Chile, Brazil and Colombia, the story was similar. Thus, the connection between political regimes and trends in inequality in Latin America is impressive. In the past 20 years, the main modern period of globalisation, however, militarism has declined in Latin America but inequality has risen in many countries. If the rise in inequality in Chile in the 1970s was due to the actions of the military, why has it not fallen more since the return of democracy?

Economic development and urbanisation in Latin America began creating a politically mobilised working class in the 1920s and 1930s, mostly integrated into political parties that were cross-class coalitions, very different from social-democratic or socialist parties in Europe. They had redistributive policies but these did not change the long-term institutional equilibrium as in Western Europe and so had little effect on inequality. Also, when real redistributive agendas emerged and even won power, as in Guatemala and Venezuela in 1945 or Chile in 1970, they provoked an anti-democratic backlash. This happened because the traditional political elites opposed democratisation in nearly all Latin American countries, typically in alliance with the military. So not only did strong socialist parties not emerge in Latin America, but when they did they were undermined by a military that tried to demobilise the left. This happened in Europe too, but not very often, probably because democracy was more of a threat to Latin American elites, whose most important asset was land, very immobile and easy to redistribute.

Rising inequality in the post-military period probably stems from structural political changes induced by military regimes when they manage to demobilise trade unions and the left, to eliminate the political base for redistributive politics. This was clearest in Chile, where inequality failed to decline following Pinochet, and in Argentina, where it rose. Such changes and ideas were also embodied in the new constitution to prevent the re-emergence of redistribution as a successful political agenda. In Argentina, the 1976-83 military regime repressed labour as ruthlessly as did the Pinochet regime. Since re-democratisation and adjustment to the debt crisis, inequality has increased under the reconstituted Peronist party, which has now dropped its redistributive agenda. Its ability to maintain its vote share regardless reflects the structural changes in Argentine society induced by the military and the debt crises. Inequality can now rise during a democratic period because one of the major coalitions in favour of redistribution has been vanquished.

This interpretation of rising and persistent inequality throws a different light on the role of neoliberalism and the range of policies connected to the Washington consensus. The mass privatisation and deregulation many Latin American countries have carried out since the 1980s must have had important effects on income distribution. Even if it was due to neoliberalism it would be hard to say what part globalisation played since trade and capital market liberalisation comes in a package with other reforms. Neoliberal economic policies may have led to increased inequality, but the Latin American military regimes changed the institutions and distribution of political power to head off future efforts at redistribution and reducing inequality. So neoliberal policies result from these new political equilibria, whether or not they actually increase inequality. Rising inequality is not clearly linked to globalisation and neoliberalism, but in OECD countries it is closely connected with labour market deregulation and in Latin America with labour repression.

What Can Be Done?

The basic cause of different levels of inequality in Latin America is lack of democracy and the nature of the party systems. In the 19th century, Latin American societies developed free from international geopolitical competition and with well-developed institutions for internal social control. The only countries that deviated from the trend of land expropriation, such as Costa Rica and Colombia, were those which had serious domestic political competition, if not full-blown democracy. During the 1970s, while inequality rose sharply in authoritarian Argentina and Chile amid policies to open the economy quickly to international economic forces, it fell in military-ruled Peru as the result of egalitarian agrarian reform. In the 1980s and 1990s, inequality rose again in many places as neoliberal economic policies were implemented, but was largely unchanged in Costa Rica and Colombia where labour market deregulation was avoided. So Latin American states and their relationship to society evolved very differently from those of East Asia or Europe, and this largely accounts for their very different levels of inequality now. Democracy has been fragile in Latin America and has yet to come up with the dramatic changes it produced in Western Europe.

How should Latin American governments respond to the challenges and opportunities of increasing globalisation? If globalisation does not by itself create inequality, what should they be doing about inequality? How could international institutions help? Many kinds of policies can cushion the impact of globalisation on inequality, but, however well intentioned, they are unlikely to be self-enforcing in Latin American political systems. Democracy seems far from consolidated there, as recent events in Peru, Paraguay, Ecuador and Venezuela show. Without belittling the recent democratic hand-over in Mexico, we should remember that Mexico has not had a single democratic election since its independence in 1821.

We could say democracy should be promoted as a "meta-institution" with big positive and normative payoffs. How could this be done? The history of conditionality on structural-adjustment lending to developing countries shows how hard it is to persuade a recalcitrant country to adopt clear economic policies. Building an accountable democracy that would empower the bottom of the income distribution seems far more complex and the theory of creating and consolidating democracy much more primitive. Building democracy also has to be in the interests of First World powers and the international institutions that hold the balance of power in the global economy. Post World War II history shows that this cannot be taken for granted. Cold-war politics sustained many oppressive and anti-democratic regimes and actively undermined Latin American democracies, notably in Guatemala in 1954 and Chile in 1973. Things have changed since 1989 but no effective and credible policy alternatives have been designed. Moving beyond this rather gloomy assessment requires much deeper understanding of the relationships between political institutions, party systems and democratic consolidation and of why the political-economy process of Western Europe has been so different from Latin America over the last 150 years.

Rapporteur's Report on Latin American Regional Session

Barbara Stallings

The papers introducing the Latin American section began with a set of facts about inequality:

— inequality in Latin America is the highest in the world;

— it has been stubbornly high and resistant to change, at least at the aggregate regional level;

— despite this regional aggregate rigidity, there have been some examples of dramatic increases in inequality in the post-war period; and

— the 1990s saw no significant improvement in distribution, and perhaps some deterioration, depending on the measures used and the countries considered.

Each of the papers offered policy proposals. Robinson proposed on the basis of his analysis that Latin America clearly needs more democracy, but he admitted that he did not have much of an idea on how to bring that about. Morley stressed the need for more rapid growth, with an emphasis on stimulating exports. Szekely argued for complementary policies to make reforms work better[1].

The interventions by civil-society participants were very concrete and focused on winners and losers. Virtually every civil-society representative argued that in Latin America in the 1990s and continuing into the current decade, there have been very few winners and many losers. Moreover, some of the losses were in absolute, not just relative, terms.

An especially vivid example of absolute loss came from one participant who spoke of the fate of poor peasants in Mexico. It involved political, economic and social exclusion of peasants, who were considered "unnecessary" for the new economic model being followed in the region. The government had decided that this group should be eliminated from the economic scene, because it was not competitive in the new world. Very closely associated with the analysis of the situation of poor peasants were indigenous groups in general. Other losers in the 1990s included informal-sector workers, many of whom had held formal-sector jobs in earlier times; women, both as producers and in home and community life; public school teachers and their students; and producers in general, who were said not to be considered in the new economic model. Small and medium enterprises in particular did not receive the support they needed and therefore could not participate in the new scheme of things.

Civil society participants had different opinions about why the region had so many losers. One explanation referred to the reforms, or the new economic model, often cited as the main cause for the plight of the losers. The main reforms mentioned were trade liberalisation, financial liberalisation, privatisation and labour market reforms. The state itself was seen as part of the problem, taking the side of the large corporations rather than the side of the majority of the people. Some interventions characterised the state as corrupt, but more typically arguments focused on the lack of democracy, the exclusion of civil society groups from participation in decision making, and the lack of local autonomy to carry out their own ideas.

The discussion of external globalisation cited, for example, unfair advantages of foreign firms and the unwillingness of industrial countries to play by their own rules. It criticised international organisations and international agreements (e.g. NAFTA, the WTO and the IMF). One person talking about NAFTA said: "We are not against opening the economies. We merely think it could be done in a better way so that more people would benefit".

Among the proposals put forward were the following:

— more democracy is needed;

— citizens need more space for participation in decision making — ordinary citizens from all parts of society;

— there should be an organised civil society to enable this participation to take place in the hoped-for new democracies;

— there should also be stronger public institutions. The state itself needs to be rebuilt, especially the justice system and social institutions. There needs to be more coherence. When the state says it wants to lower poverty, it should not be doing other things at the same time that result in increased poverty;

— particular attention needs to be paid to growth;

— there need to be guarantees for worker rights, both labour rights and social rights;

— specific programmes are needed for specific groups, especially rural producers (e.g. credit, perhaps subsidies for rural producers, but more generally the incorporation of rural development into overall national development strategies);

— there should also be support of various kinds for small and medium enterprises;

— we need to worry about the environment and sustainable development, which is part of the future of the region;

— we need to improve the situation of women, both as producers and at home and in communities;

— we need to improve both the quantity and the quality of education, especially for the lower income groups in society; and

— a monitoring mechanism of some kind is needed to guarantee that promises to effect these policies are actually carried out.

The session ended with a discussion of three points. One had to do with timing. There has not been enough time for the reforms to show that they can provide benefits for the majority of the people. While many of the reforms may have a negative impact initially, they are likely to be more positive later on. Second, the discussion mixed up long-term trends in the Latin American region with the effects of reforms. The most obvious example is a decline in the percentage of the population in the agricultural sector and perhaps in rural areas in general. This has occurred everywhere as part of the development process; it is not particularly related to the reforms. Third, despite common perceptions, there have also been losers at the top end of the income distribution. In fact, all who had special privileges under the old economic model will lose under the new situation unless they can adapt, and many of them cannot.

Note

1. The Szekely paper is not included in this volume.

PART FOUR

REGIONAL PAPERS: EAST ASIA

The Social Impact of Globalisation in Southeast Asia

Mari Pangestu

One of the biggest challenges for developing and transitional economies is how best to manage and balance the benefits of globalisation against the risks and costs. The increased competition that forces production changes in an economy will lead to better resource allocation and greater efficiency and productivity, but the net benefits are not shared equally. Some groups, sectors or regions grow much faster than others. Globalisation can do good, but the jury is still out on its social impact.

Southeast Asia has been held up as a good example of how rapid economic development can reduce income inequality and absolute poverty, but since the mid-1980s these trends have gone into reverse, especially in recent years. How did rapid liberalisation and globalisation in four of the region's major economies (Indonesia, Malaysia, Thailand and the Philippines) in the 1980s and 1990s affect growth, development, inequality and distribution? Different policies, institutions, initial conditions and investment in human and physical capital produced different results. How can we ensure that globalisation does minimal social damage?

Between 1975 and 1995, poverty fell by two-thirds in East Asia, more sharply than in any other region of the world. Life expectancy, infant mortality and access to education improved. Yet serious social problems appeared in the region before the 1997-98 economic crisis. The near-poor, those just above the poverty line, are still very numerous. Poverty is also related to urban-rural, regional, ethnic and gender differences. Less absolute poverty does not always mean more equity. The crisis underlined too that poor or vulnerable people have no social safety nets.

Opening and Globalisation

The four Southeast Asian economies were agriculture-based exporters of raw materials until the 1970s. All industrialised by import substitution (IS) then switched to exporting mainly goods intensive in unskilled labour. Import substitution often continued. When these economies began industrialising in the early 1970s, they had great poverty and inequality. During the 1970s and into the 1980s, growth was on average more than 5 per cent per annum. At first, this produced a dramatic decline in poverty in all the countries except the Philippines, but this changed between the mid-1970s and mid-1980s. Two-thirds of the region's poor still live in the countryside. Meanwhile, the urban poor have increased because of emigration to the towns. Malaysia took an early step to reduce poverty in 1971, with its New Economic Policy (NEP) aimed at "growth with equity", especially for poorer ethnic groups.

Rapid globalisation occurred from the mid-1980s to the mid-1990s when all Southeast Asian economies aggressively exported goods and shifted from labour-intensive items to those requiring more skilled labour. They also liberalised the financial sector and attracted foreign capital. Absolute poverty was now falling in all four countries. Trends in inequality were also reversed during the 1990s. In 1985-88, growth reduced poverty substantially and more than offset the increase caused by more inequitable distribution. But in 1988-91, worsening income distribution cancelled out the positive effect of growth. In 1991-94, both factors helped reduce poverty, but distribution inequality grew again in 1994-97.

The impact on the poor of the 1997 crisis that led to contraction in 1998 was compounded by drought and then heavy rains, bringing crop failures and, in Indonesia, forest fires. A political crisis aggravated the economic crisis, especially in Indonesia; it heightened social tensions caused partly by income and wealth disparities. The economic crisis worsened poverty and inequality, but the social impact was less than predicted; government action and safety-net programmes helped reduce it. Yet it was still significant and reversed the trend of declining poverty. Government cuts in basic social services spending and reduced household expenditure on health and education did not have the serious consequences feared. The effects were mixed, as health-care spending and school enrolment did not decline as sharply as expected.

The four economies had relied on a few primary commodities and agricultural exports to earn foreign exchange. Until the mid-1980s, import substitution policy modernised domestic industrial sectors to produce first consumer goods and then intermediate and capital goods. All used tariffs on finished goods, then (gradually) on intermediate and capital goods. Non-tariff barriers found increasing use. The result was a complex protection structure biased against exports and agriculture and producing manufactured goods inefficiently and expensively. Import-substituting industries located mainly in towns and engaged in capital-intensive production with less benefit to labour. Poverty and inequality reduction came more from policies of improving infrastructure and agriculture. At the same time, all four countries began encouraging an export orientation because a small domestic market limited import substitution and external developments stressed the need to earn foreign exchange. Exports first emphasised manufactures intensive in unskilled labour, largely to offset the bias against exports created by the protection system built to shield import-competing industries. Duty drawbacks or exemptions for imported inputs were introduced, along with investment incentives, export processing zones and export subsidies and credit.

All four countries had sound macroeconomic policies and kept inflation under control, except for the Philippines. Devaluation coped with current-account deficits and helped boost exports. Governments also cut budgets and tried to raise tax revenues.

The more aggressive switch to export orientations came in the mid-1980s. The four countries had been able to retain import-substitution policies much longer than the Northeast Asian economies because they could earn foreign exchange from exporting raw materials, although reliance on a narrow range of these made them vulnerable to changes in demand and prices. The world-wide recession that preceded the 1986 fall in oil prices made the need to diversify exports imperative.

From the mid-1980s, the Southeast Asian economies deregulated and liberalised trade barriers and investment restrictions. This market-oriented policy to promote exports resulted from a shift towards a "neutral" policy environment rather than favouring exports or imports, from greater trade friction with major partners (the United States and the EU) and from changes in the rules. The regulations and commitments of the GATT (now the WTO) affected the policies these countries could pursue. Major exporters found export subsidies hard to get. The region was more open to foreign investment and skilled and semi-skilled personnel. It also developed a much more market-oriented financial system, and financing through capital markets and other private sources helped fund export manufacturing and infrastructure.

Trade policy aimed chiefly at removing protection in stages, first changing non-tariff barriers to tariff equivalents and then reducing them. Streamlining customs procedures and removing other bureaucratic bottlenecks encouraged exports by eliminating extra costs for exporters who imported their inputs. Export industries continued alongside those for import substitution as trade barriers started to come down.

All the countries competed for foreign investment, thought to be important for export market access and know-how. Removal of restrictions or provision of incentives was linked to investments exporting some of their production. Deregulation included allowing almost full foreign ownership in export-oriented investments. All the economies conditioned the best incentives and the least ownership and operational restrictions on the degree of export orientation. All began to liberalise their financial sectors and capital accounts in different ways.

Outcomes

Speedy globalisation led to rapid growth of GDP and exports. The Southeast Asian economies became more part of the world economy. There were also major structural changes in domestic output. The composition of exports changed from resource-based and unskilled labour-intensive items to more skill- and capital-intensive ones, whereas in 1990, most of the countries had still depended on the old resource-based exports. The better investment climate and opening of the financial sector led to unprecedented net capital inflows, mainly to Thailand. There was also a bias towards non-traded goods such as construction, property and infrastructure. Labour's share in the agricultural and primary sectors declined. Manufacturing productivity rose faster than in agriculture, as did nominal wages, and labour markets tightened.

Major factors of the later crisis included weak financial sectors and large current-account deficits financed by short-term flows. Contagion, interaction of macroeconomic, financial and corporate weaknesses, early errors that undermined confidence and political and social crises made things worse. They showed the fragility of economies integrated with international capital markets and the importance of transparency, corporate governance and sound macroeconomic policies and financial institutions. Although the financial crisis severely affected these economies in 1998-99, none of them responded by slowing globalisation. They either contracted or grew very slowly in 1997-98. All of them, except Indonesia, grew in 1999 and seemed to be recovering. Investment shrank much more than consumption in all four countries and all had massive capital outflows.

The Social Impact

Recent studies of the effect on poverty and income distribution of opening an economy say that globalisation by itself probably does not boost growth or reduce inequality and poverty. The outcome depends on a country's resources, initial conditions, geographic location and policies accompanying the opening. Globalisation and liberalisation are not an end but a means to achieve growth with equity. Complementary policies are needed.

Problems existed during the boom years. Inequality rose in some economies, but the broad-based growth during early globalisation raised all incomes enough to stabilise or reduce inequity. Still, growth chiefly benefited urban areas and increased inequity. Social policies should have been introduced then, including access to assets, capital and education. The crisis has corrected this by hurting those who had benefited most from the boom.

Natural resources and farm sectors absorbing much of the population made for good initial conditions in these countries. Revenue from commodities was the main factor in early development, bringing in foreign exchange to pay for imports for industrialisation. The absence of a tax base at first made it also a major source of budget revenue through resource rents and taxes. The economies grew, and poverty began to decline. All four started off with unequal distributions of income, land and capital, based on regions, sectors and ethnic groups. They adopted macroeconomic stances aimed at attracting investment through stable prices and sensible monetary and fiscal policies. The focus was on infrastructure and human capital investment.

Development Policies

Import-substitution strategy created jobs, but only in urban areas. At first, protection and the bias against agriculture and exports meant that urban areas gained more from growth. This increased inequity that followed the pattern of rural-urban migration and rural development and redistribution policies.

The import substitution bias towards capital-intensive production also led eventually to unemployment. As a result, the Southeast Asian countries opted for export industries oriented in line with their comparative advantages — unskilled labour or resources. The region was also more open to foreign investment and labour, relied more on capital markets early on and had stronger trade and investment ties with the East Asian region. The second phase of export orientation, combined with greater openness to capital flows and liberalisation of the financial sector, seems to have been less equitable. Stronger growth in urban areas and non-traded sectors, and the switch from exports intensive in unskilled labour to more skill- and capital-intensive ones, led to widening disparities.

Public spending on human capital, especially provision of basic health care and education, is a key part of all these economies' efforts to help poor young people get jobs and improve themselves, thus increasing productivity and income. A focus on primary education was no problem during the first phase of export orientation because unskilled labour was needed to produce labour-intensive exports, hence reducing poverty and sometimes inequity. The second phase required more skills, so education began to matter more. The universal primary education policy led to greater inequities since the scarcity of skilled, more educated labour meant the wages of such workers rose much faster than those of the unskilled. Extra education becomes a source of mobility for the poor to raise their incomes, not just to get jobs.

Tackling rural problems is important in distributing growth more evenly in the mainly rural poverty of East and Southeast Asia. Poverty is closely tied to lack of access to farmland, and there is less of it where there are non-agricultural job opportunities. Such employment, along with land reform, developed slowly.

Social policies

The four countries had mixed success trying to correct unequal access to land and capital for rural households. Malaysia's NEP was the most comprehensive redistribution policy. Set up to tackle extreme imbalances in wealth distribution, as well as ethnic-based poverty, it dealt with the human capital issue rather than just redistributing land and wealth. The target group was then able to develop skills to make best use of their assets. The NEP averted political tension and instability, but its asset redistribution policy was less successful. None of the four economies had catch-all social security and insurance schemes to cushion unemployment, disability and ageing, although each had some kind of safety net as well as special programmes for the poor. The safety-net programmes aimed at protecting spending in key sectors such as education and health by supplying food and jobs, but setting them up hastily made them less effective. Most countries tried to improve information by conducting surveys and monitoring the impact of the financial crisis, helped by NGOs. All tried to maintain health and education spending once the IMF agreed to allow fiscal deficits instead of requiring fiscal austerity and budget surpluses. Because of weak bureaucracy and fear of leakages, different mechanisms were used. All used public works programmes to create jobs. Community investment funds also aimed to create jobs and generate infrastructure projects. None of the countries offered unemployment insurance, but all increased severance payments and encouraged self-employment. Yet limited state resources and experience meant that people ultimately relied on informal means such as extended families and informal credit.

Lessons Learned

There is no clear evidence about how globalisation affects growth, equity and poverty. The problem is that growth affects equity and vice versa. Initial conditions as well as policies have an impact on both growth and equity and it is hard to say which combination of policies best promotes them. The same set of policies interacting with different initial conditions and institutions may have different results. Globalisation will bring higher growth, more jobs and greater productivity and reduce absolute poverty. The Southeast Asian experience also supports the conventional wisdom of a broad-based strategy for reducing poverty and inequity. The major lessons are:

— At all stages of opening, sound macroeconomic conditions, especially price stability, are key for reducing poverty and inequity. All these countries have provided basic social services, funded physical and social infrastructure for areas or groups that benefit less from growth and boosted human capital through education and health services.

— Since most poor people and workers still live in the countryside, the steady decline in absolute poverty due to industrialisation shows the need to incorporate rural improvements into the development strategy. In Southeast Asia, industrialisation and most agricultural and rural development policies did not benefit the rural poor or reduce inequities as much as expected.

— Globalisation and competition mean rapid changes in sectors and in demand for skills and know-how, so flexible labour markets are important. Because Southeast Asian countries did not educate their workers fast enough, growing inequity continued owing to the sharp rise in wages of skilled compared with unskilled labour.

— The financial crisis showed how external shocks can interact with domestic vulnerabilities and lead to an economic crisis with dire social consequences. It showed that weak institutions are the main block to providing social services.

— Inequality is caused by much higher growth in towns among the skilled and in the modern capital-intensive sector. This comes from the urban focus of industrialisation with little rural-urban linkage, from levels of education and unequal access to it and from urban concentration of the boom's benefits.

— Broader access to affordable, good-quality secondary schooling is important for growth and reducing poverty and inequity.

— Poverty is declining, but not equally between income groups, town and countryside, industrial and non-industrial areas and ethnic groups. Social programmes targeting groups and areas need to be implemented. There are bound to be losers and pockets of poor people that are not reachable, so special policies must help them get out of their poverty traps.

Challenges

The Southeast Asian economies confront the rapid pace of globalisation and increased competition that will probably speed up as technology changes and excess global production capacity develops. Growth will depend on keeping their economies open and taking part in globalisation, but countries will have to learn to manage the risks of joining the world economy and the volatility of trade and capital flows. To do so, they will need sound macroeconomic management, good governance, transparency, accurate and timely information, a sound financial system and flexible factor markets.

As these countries try to soften the adverse effects of globalisation, they face other domestic challenges, such as ageing populations, more people living in towns and greater political openness and democracy. The crisis highlighted the inequities of the boom years that caused friction between regions, between the centres and local areas, between ethnic groups and between rich and poor. This has badly damaged political stability, the investment climate and overall growth. While growth is a key to reducing poverty and inequity, reducing inequalities is also crucial to promoting growth.

With more democratic participation, governments will have trouble responding to demands for greater access to education and opportunity, programmes for targeted groups and redistribution of assets or wealth. Short-term measures should be avoided as they could damage growth and efficiency, just as badly planned redistribution programmes could discourage effort and create costly bureaucracies.

What Should Countries Do?

Governments are now tackling poverty in response to greater demands by civil society. Political openness produces more pressure to ensure fairer income redistribution. Providing physical capital and infrastructure, investing in human capital (education and health) and efficiently allocating resources are necessary, but quality is key.

Government promotion of solid rural development driven by the private sector, especially through creating non-farm jobs, is important. Improving rural infrastructure and urban-rural links is better than subsidising credit or inputs. Other key issues are promoting opportunity, empowerment and enhancing security. Opportunity has to be created by investing in three kinds of assets — physical infrastructure, human capital and natural resources — and through looking after the environment. Empowerment within and between countries to ensure social inclusion and political democracy is on the rise. Social policies must now involve the wider community, not just governments. Finally, people must feel secure, helped by government policies and institutions that reduce volatility and vulnerability to economic and physical shocks. Such security comes through sound macroeconomic policies, a stronger financial system, corporate governance, transparency, the rule of law and social safety nets.

Globalisation, Liberalisation, Poverty and Income Inequality in Southeast Asia

K.S. Jomo

The World Bank said in 1993 that eight high-performing Asian economies (HPAEs) — Japan, South Korea, Chinese Taipei, Hong Kong-China, Singapore, Malaysia, Thailand and Indonesia — had achieved high, sustained and equitable export-led growth, rapid industrialisation, structural change and higher per capita incomes over the previous two decades. It said that exceptional aspects of the first five made the last three — Malaysia, Thailand and Indonesia (SEA3) — the best examples for developing countries, implying that they were comparable to the others in terms of growth, structural change, industrialisation and equity. The Bank said that the SEA3's achievements came through reducing state intervention, especially in external relations, but in fact they have not done as well at all.

Industrial policy was inferior and ill conceived in the SEA3, although some targeted government intervention did contribute to rapid growth, structural change and new internationally-competitive industries, creating jobs and boosting average incomes and thus reducing poverty. The high tide of the "East Asian Miracle" managed to lift most above the poverty line, but the effect on inequality has been more complicated.

The SEA3 grew more slowly than the other HPAEs, especially when their much higher population increase is taken into account. They are also behind in industrialisation, education and living standards. Their economic achievements have been smaller and perhaps less sustainable, judging by the greater disruption and slower recovery in Southeast Asia from the 1997-98 East Asian financial crisis. Southeast Asia has also lagged behind in democratisation, the key to sustainable, progressive social policy.

Income inequality in Malaysia and Thailand has been much greater than in the Northeast Asian three, which were helped by land redistribution in the late 1940s and early 1950s, at the beginning of the Cold War and the advent of communist regimes in neighbouring China and North Korea. Tax reform, often associated with liberalisation, has also exacerbated income inequality in the SEA3. Public spending has also probably been regressive, especially in recent years, because of declining rural development efforts after the 1970s. The ethnic parity focus in Malaysia and, to a lesser extent, Indonesia has probably also limited the impact of their redistributive efforts.

91

Rapid Growth and Open Economies

Export-led growth was supposedly the backbone of the East Asian miracle. Yet while trade liberalisation may boost some exports in the short term and may improve allocative efficiency, imports usually increase sharply too, limiting domestic demand and helping growth much less than free-trade advocates assume. What happened in the SEA3 is more like this export-led growth model than the experience of Japan, South Korea and Chinese Taipei. The latter vigorously pushed exports, while temporarily protecting domestic markets to boost their industrial and technological ability to compete internationally.

All the region's economies began their industrialisation programmes with import substitution and then moved to export orientation. In Northeast Asia, export promotion was a way to raise the international competitiveness of local industries. In the SEA3, transnational corporations set up most export-oriented industries. International trends and pressures have made trade liberalisation inevitable and changes in international trade rules mean many instruments can no longer be used by governments. Local content requirements, for example, were phased out with the Uruguay Round of GATT negotiations. Trade policy can still be used to support industrial policy, however.

Southeast Asian HPAEs have relied much more on foreign direct investment (FDI) than Japan, South Korea and Chinese Taipei, raising questions about their industrial and technological capabilities and the sustainability of their growth and industrialisation. Foreign financial capital developed close relations with politically powerful *rentiers* and encouraged financial liberalisation in the region. Capital inflows — mainly in the form of private bank borrowings and portfolio investments from abroad — financed current account deficits and had mixed consequences for economic growth.

The changing positions of these countries in the world economy have also had adverse effects on the SEA3. High growth and rapid industrialisation from the late 1980s until the 1997-98 financial crises were due to policies that made the region attractive for industrial capital relocating from elsewhere in the region. By the mid-1990s, the SEA3 had become far less attractive for low-cost production, but had not developed enough to make further technological progress on their own, and their exports had become less competitive. Rapid growth got temporary sustenance from massive capital flows into the region, which reversed in 1997.

The Southeast Asian crisis can also be blamed on poorly organised financial liberalisation that brought massive but easily reversible capital inflows into the region. They boosted spending through increased domestic investment, but also fed consumption booms and speculation. The resulting greater external deficit was not sustainable, and capital fled. The crisis was not due, in itself, to macroeconomic profligacy or cronyism. Financial markets and the IMF accelerated a lack of investor confidence in the region and the IMF's drastic measures deepened the recession and threw millions of people into poverty.

The World Bank's 1993 *East Asian Miracle* report encouraged the belief in egalitarian export-oriented growth in the region by claiming that growth led to low inequality in the HPAEs. In fact there is no clear link and no declining income inequality, but the success of the five East Asian economies in reducing poverty has nevertheless been spectacular.

Redistribution and Human Resources

Land reform has been less important in the resource-rich Southeast Asian economies, where politics discouraged redistribution and greater resource wealth weakened the pressure to industrialise. No major redistributive land reforms occurred in Malaysia, but the government boosted rural, especially land development with its New Economic Policy in 1971 to narrow ethnic disparities and reduce poverty. The five governments also introduced social safety nets to soften the effect of rapid structural changes and cyclical influences. Reduction of poverty and income inequality can thus accompany and even help rapid growth and industrialisation, while income inequalities tend to worsen with economic liberalisation, especially without redistribution efforts.

The East Asian miracle is often described as anchored in efforts to improve the region's human resources, but in the Southeast Asian HPAEs, investment in education has been very much less than elsewhere and does not seem to have been crucial to the region's speedy growth and industrialisation. Future rapid structural change, industrialisation and productivity gains may not be sustainable as a result. Investment in human resources probably has helped reduce poverty and inequality. South Korea and Chinese Taipei now have highly educated labour forces and primary education has been universal there since the 1960s. Achievements in secondary and tertiary education have been far smaller in Malaysia, Thailand and Indonesia. Rapid growth, more education and falling unemployment have pushed up real wages in these economies despite the weakness of trade unions, which have to cope with government hostility. The three countries have sought industrial investment by emphasising cheap labour, which hampers rapid wage growth.

Economic Liberalisation and Inequality

After the fiscal and foreign debt crises of the 1980s, most governments emerged leaner, partly because of economic liberalisation. Government spending fell, public-sector expansion was reversed, state-owned enterprises were curbed and privatisation was pursued. Government regulations were cut back to encourage private investment. The process often damaged economic welfare.

South Korea and Chinese Taipei lack natural resources, but have transformed their economies through interventionist industrial policies. Malaysia, Thailand and Indonesia have relied more on resource rents than growth to alleviate poverty. Export-oriented industrialisation, driven primarily by foreign capital in Southeast Asia, has helped reduce unemployment and thus raise household incomes. East Asian economies seem to have managed to grow rapidly without seriously worsening income distribution, and both urban and rural poverty have continued to decline. All governments had policies to combat poverty and improve income distribution.

Rising income inequality has re-emerged with liberalisation since the 1980s. Deregulation, less government intervention, less commitment to earlier redistributive mechanisms and greater government efforts to help investors have probably all contributed, and things are likely to get worse. How can a decline in poverty and inequality be sustained amid pressures for trade, financial and investment liberalisation, especially since the 1997-98 crisis? Efforts to help the poor with land reform, subsidised housing and access to education have all helped. Liberalisation of agricultural trade, especially food, should be gradual because cheap food imports will destroy the livelihoods of many farmers. Governments should develop alternative employment. New kinds of indirect subsidies may compensate for direct ones that may be hard to maintain in the new trade environment. More government education and training will make firms and economies more competitive and reduce income inequality.

Labour market liberalisation in Southeast Asia has increased labour flexibility without improving worker security. Some of this flexibility has come from changing international production relations, but governments wanting to lure investment and boost growth have pushed much of it. Weak trade unions and labour laws have worsened the plight of the region's workers and perhaps income distribution. Unions should be encouraged to work with management and government to increase social corporatism, because enhanced trust, commitment and efficiency boost competitiveness and make wage increases possible. Growth should become a shared responsibility, benefiting all parties. As traditional industrial policies are increasingly sidelined, there will be a rare opportunity for human development, social policy and redistribution proponents. The danger is that only measures seen to support short-term economic growth and industrialisation will be adopted. Long-term progress in health, education and productivity will be needed to sustain growth and improve living standards.

Public Policy and Income Distribution

It is not clear that the SEA3's policies softened globalisation's effect on income inequality and poverty. Rapid export-led growth in the region reduced unemployment and raised incomes, so poverty was significantly reduced, but the effect on income inequality is ambiguous.

Did some East Asian countries pursue liberalisation in a way more beneficial to the poor and if so, why? All the governments were authoritarian until the 1990s, but securing legitimacy and popular backing were nearly always important. In Malaysia, the authorities began rural reforms in the 1950s, first to counter communist influence and then to secure the key ethnic-Malay rural vote. This official commitment to redistribution has helped. In Indonesia, generous foreign aid and windfall oil rents from the mid-1970s provided money for government programmes to win over the rural poor by achieving rice self-sufficiency and facilitating migration involving new rural land development. In Thailand, rapid growth without significant official redistribution efforts also dramatically reduced poverty while income inequalities continued to grow. There is little evidence of significant policies in the East Asian region to compensate for the effects of liberalisation. The major policies involved new infrastructure, investment incentives and human resource development. There were fewer such efforts in Southeast Asia, except in Singapore and Malaysia.

Fiscal systems do not seem to have had a progressive impact and the tax burden has regressed from direct to indirect taxes. Overall public spending does not seem to have been progressive either. In Latin America, capital market and capital account liberalisation increased inequality by raising returns to asset holders. With industry in Southeast Asia dominated by FDI, domestic financial interests gained influence over financial liberalisation, ensuring it was in their own interests. This resulted in considerable abuse and made national financial systems vulnerable.

The conditions attached to the emergency credit facilities the IMF gave Thailand, Indonesia and South Korea not only exacerbated their crises, but also sought further to liberalise their economies. The Bretton Woods institutions have discouraged East Asian governments from developing Western-style welfare institutions, instead favouring social safety nets, especially in crises. This is ironic. While developing countries have been discouraged from making selective state interventions such as industrial policy because their governments are deemed to lack the capacity for effective targeting, such targeting is favoured for the far more difficult job of identifying the poor in crisis situations.

What Can Be Done?

Growth and distribution are frequently seen as trade-offs. Rents and rent seeking are often rejected as being linked with corruption and thus undesirable on moral and efficiency grounds. They should be reconsidered in developing an alternative approach to growth and distribution in the face of liberalisation and globalisation, and as a redistributive key to maintaining the social order, providing incentives, developing capabilities or allocating resources needed for growth. After two decades, a critical review of the Washington Consensus, which sees no alternative to liberalisation and globalisation, is long overdue. International financial liberalisation has been bad not only for redistribution but also for growth. It has not only failed to ensure that funds keep moving from the capital rich to the capital poor, but has increased the real costs of finance, while increasing systemic volatility and vulnerability, exerting contractionary or deflationary macroeconomic pressures and curbing selective government intervention to enhance development.

Trade liberalisation may theoretically improve overall consumer welfare, but in the short and medium term it has caused massive job and income losses. Investment liberalisation too has systematically reduced possible gains from foreign direct investment to the host economy. The new international economic regime also limits development initiatives. There are strong reasons to doubt liberalisation's and globalisation's allegedly benign consequences for growth as well as distribution. High growth in East Asia has been due to successful public policy interventions, especially selective industrial policy, rather than economic liberalisation. South Korea and Chinese Taipei have not only achieved far more growth, industrialisation and structural change than Thailand, Indonesia and Malaysia, but inequality has been much lower too. Liberalisation has, in fact, undermined their ability to catch up. The most urgent medium-term task is creating such new capacities in the current conditions of accelerated liberalisation and globalisation and the IMF-imposed reforms. Economic liberalisation in recent years has coincided with and perhaps worsened inequality in all countries since the 1980s.

The changed international investment climate (especially in East Asia), with accelerated globalisation and economic integration over the last decade, poses new challenges for investment regimes. Investment policy reform was already under way in the region before the 1997-98 crises, taking into consideration the fresh constraints imposed by new international regulations and commitments, as well as the more sophisticated industries desired by some of these economies. The crisis and its aftermath, including the conditions imposed by the IMF on Thailand and Indonesia for emergency credit facilities, have also introduced new constraints. Attracting new green-field investments to restore and sustain growth as well as structural change is all the more urgent as a lot more of the recent FDI has involved acquisitions.

Domestic political priorities in the region have often neglected or limited technology policies, which have not been sensitive enough to sector or industry conditions. The scope for discretionary policies has become reduced as global regulations are defined by international organisations that can enforce them. Changing international economic governance has strengthened transnational corporate claims to intellectual property rights, raising the costs and reducing the likelihood of the international technology transfer so crucial to earlier experiences of late industrialisation, but there is still scope in the region for sound technology policies.

How can better conditions be created for making and implementing good policy? Much needs to be done to ensure greater competence, transparency and accountability. If a government lacks human resources, consultancy services can be bought on the market. They rarely involve accountability, however, so new mechanisms must ensure more of it among both policy makers and those providing technical and other inputs. Most of all, there must be a clear rejection of the Washington Consensus and its false premise that there is no alternative. In September 2000, just before the Prague annual meetings of the IMF and World Bank, the Fund's new managing director, Horst Köhler, announced that the IMF would, from then, present governments with a set of policies

— and likely consequences — that they could choose from. This would be a major change because developing countries have increasingly confronted imposed policies determined by organisations reflecting vested interests.

Some international economic liberalisation is inevitable, so sequencing issues need to be considered, along with pro-active initiatives or supply responses. Developing countries are barely equipped to deal with the many complications and details of globalisation. Solidarity and co-operation among their governments have declined significantly since the 1970s, especially on economic issues, just when they have been most needed. The sympathy of some European governments for their development aspirations has also declined. Both kinds of co-operation and mutual support must be restored if a viable alternative to the emerging *status quo* is to have any chance. Recent initiatives such as the Asia-Europe Forum offer such a prospect, but much more progress is needed. The existence of international forums, however, including ostensibly democratic ones, does not in itself ensure that developing country interests will be best served, as seen recently with the World Trade Organisation.

Caution is needed about lessons to be drawn from particular experiences. This does not mean no lessons at all can be drawn, but there is a tendency to abstract for emulation models that often ignore crucial variables, making them fairly useless for policy making. Creatively combining and tailoring lessons from other experiences is often better. This requires great knowledge and considerable modesty about prospects for their successful application.

Rapporteur's Report on East Asian Session

S. Mansoob Murshed

The regional breakout session was chaired by Shoji Nishimoto of the Asian Development Bank (ADB). He began his remarks on the effects of globalisation on poverty and income distribution by emphasising the need for growth to be pro-poor and development broad-based, in line with the institutional mission of his and many other multilateral international agencies.

Both of the paper presentations had a great deal in common, especially in connection with their central message regarding the Southeast Asian development experience. Both focused on Southeast Asia, more specifically Indonesia, Malaysia and Thailand. Mari Pangestu began by sketching the overall picture regarding inequality and poverty in Southeast Asia. Most countries had achieved remarkable success, relative to other parts of the developing world, in reducing poverty. She did, however, add a cautionary note regarding the definition of poverty. If another group — the near-poor — were taken into account there could be an 11 per cent to 25 per cent increase in poverty. The picture regarding inequality was rather different. In Thailand, for example, growth had been accompanied by a rise in inequality. Consequently, growth and not redistributive tendencies drove the reduction in poverty. She also emphasised the growing urban-rural divide in the region.

Mari Pangestu mentioned the three stages of globalisation in East Asia. The first involved manufactured exports intensive in semi-skilled or unskilled labour. Poverty declined in Indonesia, Malaysia and Thailand, but inequality rose initially in all three countries. In Thailand it continued to increase because of the absence of redistributive policies. Surplus rural labour got absorbed into urban sectors. Overall this stage was both pro-poor and pro-female. The second stage in the experience with globalisation involved exporting more technologically superior manufactured goods (mainly electronics) from the mid-1980s. This was driven by inward investment from Northeast Asia, where exchange-rate appreciation and rising labour costs induced some outward relocation of production. In Southeast Asia skill shortages and rising inequality accompanied this stage. The third stage, during the 1990s, involved financial liberalisation and foreign bank lending. Asset price inflation led the boom in some cases. "Cronyism" grew and standards of governance declined. Eventually the unsustainability of this process, which involved current-account deficits financed by capital account surpluses in combination with fixed exchange rates, led to the crash of 1997 and the spread of financial contagion in the region.

Although recovery is progressing, and growth is back on track, the experience highlighted the increased vulnerability of certain social groups. Social protection for these groups is of paramount importance. In Thailand and Indonesia social safety nets were a comparative failure, as they often did not reach the poor, with a leakage rate of about 30 per cent. Furthermore, the need to improve governance and institutional capacity is also crucial at the present juncture.

Jomo's paper emphasised the same points. His presentation put great emphasis on the differences between Northeast and Southeast Asia. The crucial difference lay in the initial conditions in the two regions prior to the contemporary experience of growth and take-off. South Korea, Chinese Taipei and even Japan pursued a policy of asset redistribution vigorously after World War II. The Cold-war climate and the threat of communism in the neighbourhood (from China and North Korea) were central to these redistributive policies. Another major difference lay in the differing roles of foreign direct investment (FDI). Whereas Southeast Asia has placed continuing reliance on FDI in domestic production, Northeast Asia placed greater emphasis on other means of technology transfer that involved domestic ownership. Jomo pointed out that WTO rules on intellectual property (TRIPs) make the Northeast Asian experience of technology transfer difficult to emulate. Singapore's heavy reliance on FDI had a strategic and political motivation in the initial period following its separation from Malaysia. Industrial policy was more pro-active and superior in Northeast than in Southeast Asia, and import protection at the early stages of industrialisation was more common.

Consequently, Jomo argued that Northeast Asia had more development-oriented states. Yet there were successes in Southeast Asia, the most important of which involved the efficient management of natural resource revenues and the avoidance of harmful "Dutch disease" effects in agriculture and manufacturing, particularly in Indonesia. Indonesia channelled revenues during the oil boom era into agrarian reform and internal migration. Malaysia had redistributive policies favouring ethnic Malays, including a hefty element of social policy in the health and education sectors. This has had major beneficial spin-offs. Also, the harmful effects of ethnic fractionalisation on growth, as suggested by Easterly and Levine for Africa, were avoided. Only 10 per cent of overall inequality in Malaysia could be explained along ethnic lines.

Jomo stressed that the much-vaunted East Asian developmental model as an example for other developing regions is limited and flawed in many respects. He added that recovery following the 1997 crisis was more robust in Malaysia and South Korea, which followed more reflationary policies, unlike Indonesia and Thailand, which remained more at the mercy of the IMF.

Moving on to the contributions and interventions by representatives of civil society, Mokhtar Pakpahan (Indonesian trade union leader) emphasised that trade union rights were far better enshrined in the Philippines than in Indonesia, particularly during the Suharto period. He bemoaned that ILO conventions were still not honoured in his country. He also added that, unfortunately, the IMF and the World Bank were more influential in Indonesia compared with other countries in the region. This reduced the room for manoeuvre in domestic policy making.

Ernesto Arellano (Philippines, trade unionist) described the problems of his country, particularly the difficulties associated with shifting comparative advantage, which was making his country progressively less attractive to inward investors in labour-intensive exports such as garments and leather goods. Despite liberalisation, deregulation and privatisation, the Philippines economy was failing to diversify. Many export-oriented sectors based on inward investment were relocating to other countries in the region, such as China and Vietnam. Despite a perception that labour is more militant in the Philippines, the real culprit could be the poor infrastructure. Because of the gradual decline in some export-oriented manufacturing sectors, trade union membership had fallen from 43 000 to 18 000. There was an increased movement to greater labour market "flexibility" and "contractualisation" with, in general, a loss of jobs accompanied by declining real wages and repression of workers.

Ravadee Prasertcharoensuk (Thai NGO-COD) spoke about the rural poor in Thailand. She expressed her doubts regarding the official poverty-line definitions. She stressed that inequality was increasing, and agricultural exports occurred at the expense of food security for the poor. The growth of agribusinesses marginalised poorer farmers. She questioned the positive link between growth and globalisation, claiming that it raised dependency and was inimical to the interests of the poor. She claimed that the international governance structure and loan/aid conditionality were bad for the poor.

The floor discussion surrounded issues regarding foreign direct investment, policy failure and the origins of the 1997 financial crisis. Mekvichai Banasopit (Bangkok City government) outlined policies of the Bangkok City government towards a floating population of 6 million to 15 million inhabitants. Despite urban poverty, there is a high propensity towards urban migration. Many of the urban poor leave the city during difficult economic circumstances for rural areas, only to return to Bangkok because the only possible jobs are located there.

Thuraisingham Indrani (Malaysia, SEA Food Security Council) spoke of the relationship between national food security and globalisation. The most pressing problem for marginalised farmers in her country, many of whom are active in commodity agriculture, is the insecurity of land tenure. There is a great deal of illegal occupation of land. Landlessness grew as foreign companies purchased land from the poor for various purposes (including golf courses). Government policies are failing this group, with no cogent steps taken to reabsorb these families into other sectors of the economy. She emphasised the disproportionate but unrecognised contribution of women in agriculture. She also called for developing countries to form coalitions in the sphere of agriculture in forthcoming WTO negotiations.

Leonardo Montemayor (Philippines, Member of Parliament and representative of free farmers) stressed that in general the problem of poverty deserved greater attention from policy makers, relative to concerns about inequality. The agricultural sector in his country is in a precarious situation despite tariff protection. In any case tariff protection has been gradually declining and would have to be removed in order to be compliant with AFTA rules. Domestic food production is uncompetitive and the threat of cheaper imports is a real danger to domestic food producers. The answer to their problems lies in improved productivity. He concluded by stating that globalisation is a double-edged sword, and that countries and societies needed to prepare for its effects.

Lisa Isa (Indonesia, FOKUBA) spoke of greater labour flexibility seriously undermining and disadvantaging workers in Indonesia, not just the poorest of the poor. She stressed the importance of adhering to ILO core labour standards and the absence of adequate social protection in her country.

The floor discussion recognised that globalisation produces both winners and losers. It called, however, for globalisation with a human face. This calls for needed pro-poor policies and social protection. Globalisation should not bring about a set of *reductio ad absurdum* policies exclusively on the supply side, but must enhance domestic institutions and capacities. Equally, the system of global governance and the existing international financial architecture need reform, so that they are less inimical to the interests of developing countries and the poor. Globalisation in Asia, as elsewhere, produces a backlash among the losers, as the gainers do not compensate them. Despite scepticism regarding the East Asian developmental paradigm and the "flying geese" pattern of development, it was recognised that the region, contrary to the predictions of Myrdal in the 1960s, was after all the most successful developing region in the world in achieving growth along with poverty reduction.

PART FIVE

CONCLUDING REMARKS

Globalisation and Free Cars: A Parable

Richard Kohl

One of the points of this dialogue was to bring to the OECD people who don't normally participate in OECD meetings. We don't usually include stakeholders from developing countries, at least not in such large numbers, from so many countries and from so many diverse backgrounds — farmers, union activists, women entrepreneurs, NGO leaders. The goal was to include those who have been excluded from international forums like this. The idea was to *listen* —

— to what stakeholders had to tell us about how globalisation has affected them;

— to what they think needs to be done about globalisation;

— to what kinds of assistance stakeholders need;

— to what kinds of research will help them cope with globalisation; and

— to what kinds of changes need to be made in the policies of OECD countries and international institutions.

Bringing all of you and listening to you may seem like a small thing, but this was a big experiment for the OECD and a successful one. We hope that for all of you it was an opportunity to exchange views with each other, learn from each other, make some contacts and network, and that you will be able to build on that in the future.

Let us talk for a minute about language, communication and globalisation. As part of this experiment, we've had several different groups participating, people from many different countries speaking a number of languages. More important, we've had economists and non-economists present and discovered that they don't speak the same language. Everybody has been trying very hard to overcome this, admirably, but it has made communication very difficult. We could arrange for interpretation in English, Spanish, French and sometimes some Portuguese, but forgot to arrange for interpretation from "economese", the specialised language of Ph.D. economists and policy makers, to the language of daily conversation, to the vernacular. Since most of you who have come from developing countries have already had to suffer a little bit of cultural imperialism and learn a European language to be here, it is incumbent upon us, the economists, to be able to speak to you in your language. We must do a better job of this in the future.

Communication relates to globalisation both positively and negatively. Many of you are here largely because of globalisation. Your voices have been heard these last two days precisely because you have been excluded from globalisation, because you haven't been heard in the past. Yet we were able to contact most of you because of globalisation, by internet, fax or telephone calls; that probably couldn't have been done, or afforded, ten or 20 years ago. On the other hand, a lot of people are not here, and most of them are the real poor. We did not ask for income statements, but suspect that most of you don't make less than a dollar a day. The real poor are not here because we couldn't reach them by e-mail or fax, or because they don't usually speak a European language — and frankly, we didn't have enough money to provide translation into Thai, Indonesian and other non-European languages. Thus, we tried to be as inclusive as we could, but we didn't get as far as we'd like and will try harder in the future.

In an attempt to communicate a little bit better today, you will now get a story rather than some economic lessons, a story about cars. Once upon a time, probably in the last 15 years, there was a car manufacturer somewhere in the South, in a developing country. It was probably, in fact, a foreign investor with a commitment to corporate social responsibility. This company decided — we don't know the motivation — to give free cars to 99 people in the country where their plant was located. Six months later, the company wanted to do a follow-up study on the cars, an impact assessment. They found out that one-third of the recipients of the cars, 33 of them, used their cars all the time. They drove everywhere and as a result their lives seemed to be much better. Another third, again 33 people, did not use their cars at all and were pretty much the same as they were before they got the cars. Another third were either injured or dead from car accidents.

How do we explain this? An analyst working for the car manufacturer reviewed the data, saw that two-thirds of the people were either better off or just the same and concluded that the car give-away was a clear success. Since economists are naturally sceptical about these things, an independent economist decided to analyse the data on the impact of the car give-away using sophisticated statistical analysis — some of the same techniques that economists use to study the impact of globalisation. Because a third were better off, a third were worse off, and a third were about the same, the statistical analysis showed that *on average*, the car give-away had no effect; no systematic relationship appeared between receiving a car and people's quality of life. Finally, a civil society NGO decided to do their own analysis, focused on the third of the recipients injured or dead from car accidents. They determined that the car give-away had been a disaster, yet another example of how multinational corporations hurt people in developing countries.

All three of these approaches are mistaken, whether applied to free cars or to globalisation, because they ask the wrong question. The right one is, "How do we explain what happened to each of the three groups?" Certainly we need to focus particularly on the third that died, but we also want to find out what happened to the other two-thirds, because the goal is to get everybody into that first group.

So, what actually happened to each of those three groups? Why were some people better off? It turns out that they knew how to drive; they had money to buy fuel, and they had the political influence to have roads built to their houses. Probably they were rich. What happened to those for whom nothing changed, who didn't use their cars? Most of them didn't know how to drive. They couldn't afford the lessons and costs of getting a driving licence or didn't have enough money to buy fuel. Others didn't have enough political influence to get roads built to their homes or couldn't afford the tolls on newly built private highways.

The most important story is what happened to those who were injured or killed. Some of them didn't know how to drive and couldn't afford to learn. Yet they drove anyway because they couldn't afford to live close to their work, they had to go very far to earn a living and this was the only way they could get to work. Some were hit by huge trucks that came from the North, trucks going too fast on poor roads with no speed limits. If there were such limits, they were able to bribe the police and didn't have to obey. Some were hurt or killed because their free cars had safety flaws, and the safety standards that the manufacturer had to comply with were much weaker than those in its home country.

How does this relate to globalisation, to what we have been hearing from stakeholders from developing countries? They have been saying that globalisation, liberalisation, is happening in their countries without adequate preparation and without their participation. If one can summarise their comments in four categories, globalisation is occurring without *GCARs* — *G*overnance, *C*apacity building, *A*ccess to infrastructure, markets and inputs, and access to *R*esources like land and education. Because of this, globalisation at best leaves a lot of people out; at worst it creates a lot of poverty and vulnerability. Stakeholders have said here that they aren't against globalisation, but they want to participate, to be included. Inclusion doesn't just mean in the global economy. They want a say in the rules, in designing domestic policies, in negotiating in multilateral accords, in bargaining with international institutions.

This means that, contrary to the conventional wisdom in development economics and the donor community, policies for governance, capacity building, access and redistribution are not complementary. They are basic. Political participation by stakeholders is not window dressing to legitimise what technocrats will do anyway; it is an essential part of policy making. GCARs and participation are not like the coffee and mint you get after dinner. They are the foundations of the meal, the meat and potatoes, the rice and fish.

To bring all this back to the story about free cars, capacity building means you have to teach people how to drive so that they can get to work without being killed. Access means that there must be roads to everybody's house. Resources means that people need enough money to buy fuel or maybe even their own cars. Governance means making cars safe wherever they're built, regulating the size and speed of trucks that use the roads and giving local people who live near these roads and use them every day a say in those regulations. It also means providing equal access. If the big trucks from the North get to come down on the roads in the South, then the cars in the South must be able to go north on the same roads.

One last point, which the women in the room already know. Many of those hurt and killed actually were women. Why? They were less likely to know how to drive because of discrimination in the educational system, because their husbands wouldn't let them take lessons or because they had no control over the family finances, even if they earned the money. They had to drive anyway to ensure enough food on the table to feed their children.

What lessons does this little story have for research and policy on how to improve globalisation, to get inclusive, pro-poor globalisation? First, in assessing the impact of globalisation, economists will have to go beyond statistical analysis and the average results, and look instead at the experience of each country and individual groups within countries, especially gender groups. Second, we have to globalise more carefully. We have to be prepared for globalisation, not just let it happen. We have to customise trade and capital accounts for liberalisation to each country's circumstances. Liberalisation has to be part of an overall pro-poor strategy in which "complementary" reforms are basic. Policy — GCARs — will be designed to get everybody in the better group and will make sure that those policies are particularly targeted to include women. Third, the state in developing countries must still have a role; the market has a valuable purpose, but it can't deliver governance, capacity building, access and redistribution. The state must do this. Finally, how do we get developing countries, OECD governments and international agencies to implement the right policies? Part of the process involves dialogues like this one. The poor need a voice, a seat at the table. We have made an important beginning. Now we need to go forward so that we can all benefit from globalisation.

Conclusions to the Conference Volume

Richard Kohl

The dialogue was a success in terms of both product and process. The research results, presented over 20 papers, examined trends in poverty and inequality globally and within individual regions and countries and analysed the impact of globalisation on those variables. The papers and reports in this volume give a good sense of the debate and of developments in inequality, external integration, domestic liberalisation and the policy response in the three regions covered in the dialogue. They provide a powerful synthesis of our understanding to date of the effects of globalisation on inequality in developing countries.

Before turning to the content, a few remarks on process are called for. With the papers as background, the dialogue itself was very productive. It was particularly noteworthy in that it extended even further the Centre's tradition of inclusion by giving a voice to those largely excluded in the past from the meetings of international organisations. Of the nearly 160 people who came, nearly 50 were stakeholders from developing countries in Southeast Asia, sub-Saharan Africa and Latin America. They participated alongside policy makers, experts and researchers from the OECD and the South.

More discussions are clearly needed between stakeholders, experts and policy makers from the North and South on the subject of globalisation and inequality. The dialogue provided an important first step. It also illuminated a number of difficulties for process and organisation. The meeting was organised along the lines of an academic-style conference, with formal panels and papers. Interventions by experts were often too technical and inaccessible to stakeholders. For their part, stakeholders tended to make set statements and to focus on problems rather than solutions. That the meeting was very large inhibited creation of a more informal environment conducive to real discourse, and the use of formal panels divided "experts" and stakeholders. These problems could be resolved in future encounters by changing the number of participants, and reorienting the format towards workshops, with research and papers in a more supporting role. An additional improvement would be to link dialogues to follow-up activities to provide for continuity and help build a global community. A series of regular dialogues on specific aspects of globalisation would be ideal.

Trends in Income Inequality and Poverty

The opening session of the meeting covered world trends in inequality and poverty in both OECD and developing countries, and their connection to globalisation. Regional dialogues followed. Developments in national and global poverty and inequality have been an ongoing subject of tremendous debate, and this was true of the Paris dialogue as well. In large part, debate occurs because income distribution data are poor and inconsistent in coverage, and surveys are all too infrequent. This makes it difficult to assess accurately what is happening in individual countries, let alone the developing world, and to confirm to what extent anecdotal impressions of changes in poverty inequality are borne out by statistical measures, especially in the poorest countries. Assessing any causal role for globalisation in these developments becomes even more complicated because the dates of relevant income or expenditure surveys do not always nicely bracket major changes in policy or openness.

Evidence from the University of Texas Inequality Project (UTIP) shows clearly that in many middle and upper income countries a substantial widening in wage differentials between skilled and unskilled workers has occurred since the late 1970s, particularly in OECD countries, Latin America and East Asia. The period corresponded to the period of globalisation. There was much greater disagreement as to changes in income inequality, let alone its links to globalisation. Whether wage inequality translates into rising income inequality depends on what is happening to the supply of skilled workers and demographic factors such as household size and women's labour force participation. The evidence presented for the OECD countries shows that between the mid-1980s and the late 1990s inequality had clearly risen in the transition economies and in some OECD Members, but not in others. One discussant argued forcefully that in OECD member countries, changes in labour market institutions and the social safety net were key, and that these tended to be discontinuous policy shocks rather than changes in some trend. At the same time, it was noted that small changes in poverty statistics can conceal tremendous underlying changes. After the Russia crisis in 1996 poverty increased by 2 percentage points, but this was a net result of 18 per cent of the population falling into poverty and 16 per cent escaping from it.

The presentation comparing current and 19th century globalisation showed that inequality has probably widened in a slight majority of developing countries since the early 1980s. It has remained the highest in the world in Latin America and in several cases is rising. In Southeast Asia, inequality also began to increase in the late 1980s in several countries, even before the East Asia crisis of 1997, a reversal of decades of progress. Sub-Saharan Africa has seen progress in a few countries. The general picture seems to be one of at best maintaining high if not increasing levels of inequality between the mid-1980s and early 1990s. There is too little recent evidence for that region to discuss trends in inequality in the 1990s. The slowdown in growth clearly hindered progress in reducing poverty, as Table 3 shows. Absolute income poverty increased in both Latin America and sub-Saharan Africa, with only modest progress in South Asia.

Table 3. **Poverty Rates in Developing Regions, 1987-96**
(Change in absolute poverty, 1987-96, in percentage points)

	Low Incomes		
	$1 per person/day	$2 per person/day	Poverty gap
Latin America	+0.3	+1.5	0
Sub-Saharan Africa	+1.9	+0.3	+2.5
East Asia	-11.7	-18.4	-2.8
South Asia	-2.7	-1.0	-1.4

Source: Poverty figures are from Kohl and O'Rourke (2000), Table 19, based on Chen and Ravallion (1999) and the authors' calculations. Poverty gap is a measure of the average distance in percentage points between the mean consumption level of those below the poverty line (here $1/day) and the poverty line itself.

The Effects of Globalisation

Linking globalisation to movements in inequality and poverty is extremely difficult. In contrast to the late 19th century, several aspects of the current globalisation probably contribute to greater inequality in many countries. International factor price equalisation in the late 19th century relied heavily on labour migration, which had an equalising effect on inequality in the peripheral countries of that period. Since the 1970s, trade, capital and technology flows have been relatively much more important than labour migration, and, given OECD immigration policies, what (legal) South to North migration is occurring has favoured skilled labour. This and other factors have created a unified world market in skilled labour and probably driven up skilled wages globally. At the same time, as Adrian Wood (1994, 1997) has suggested, there has been a substantial increase in the world supply of low-skilled and unskilled labour with the increased integration of China and India into the world economy, putting downward pressure on unskilled wages. Taken together, changes in the world supply of unskilled labour and integration of skilled labour markets can probably explain a large part of the widening in global wage differentials found in the UTIP data.

Another characteristic of the current globalisation is that prospects for growth have diverged markedly across developing countries. The global environment has not favoured the low-income and the least-developed countries, which export mostly primary products and low-skill-intensive manufactures. Markets in the North, for instance, have been much more closed to these categories of Southern exports, while often selling excess agricultural production on the world markets. The global environment has also made it difficult for the majority of countries to move up in their product niches. While manufactures account for roughly 80 per cent of developing country exports, only a very few of the richest middle income countries have been able to shift fully towards manufacturing exports and move up the value-added chain. These have tended to be the countries geographically close to the three key OECD markets (Central Europe, Mexico, East Asian NICs), allowing for very close integration into production systems.

111

Invariably these same countries are the major recipients of FDI and capital inflows. Capital flows have been highly concentrated towards the richest developing countries, thus widening the income gap with lower-income countries. These flows have been highly concentrated within countries as well, and tend to favour skilled over unskilled labour, increasing domestic wage inequality. The presentation on labour's share of national income showed that the labour share had fallen substantially in a large number of developing countries, and this clearly correlated with the experience of balance-of-payments crises, indirectly implicating greater capital flows.

Regional and Country Effects

Despite the difficulties, the papers in this volume give a very thorough and comprehensive review of developments in Latin America, sub-Saharan Africa and Southeast Asia in terms of inequality, external integration, domestic liberalisation and the policy response. The general conclusion is that globalisation is increasing inequality in many developing countries, but that the effects tend to be small and other, largely domestic factors have much more importance. This is confirmed in the two papers in this volume on Latin America, which summarise the results of a large number of country case studies and panel econometric studies. Their reviews of the evidence show that the effects of globalisation on inequality were small and mixed, the positive and negative effects largely offsetting. The study of labour shares in the South found that they fell with cuts in government spending and increased with greater trade openness, both standard components of structural adjustment packages. By contrast, the imposition of capital account restrictions helps maintain the labour share once financial crises occur. Similar conclusions are presented in the Southeast Asia and sub-Saharan Africa papers. These conclusions were consistent with the findings from analysis of the WIDER Income Inequality data; that work shows that capital account liberalisation and tax reforms tend to widen inequality, trade liberalisation seems to have no effect, and privatisation often improves inequality. The WIDER studies find, in contrast to much of the work presented in this volume, that these globalisation-related factors account for much of the increased inequality that occurred in developing countries in the last 15-20 years[1].

Even if it is correct on average that the effects of globalisation on inequality and poverty are small and offsetting, this does not mean, as some authors (Dollar and Kraay, 2000) suggest, that globalisation is not having any effect on inequality or growth. The average hides a great deal of variance, with large positive effects in some countries and negative effects in others. It suggests that the impact of global forces and specific reforms on individual economies depends on the particular characteristics of a country. These include its relative factor abundance and niche in the world economy; the extent of distortions to its production structure and its distribution of assets; the way the country has integrated into the world economy or liberalised; and the strength and completeness of domestic institutions responsible for resource allocation.

Where globalisation has tended to increase inequality and poverty is most often where it has amplified pre-existing inequalities in the distribution of productive assets and magnified the effects of institutional weaknesses and rigidities. Particularly important are the underlying distribution of land and human capital, the educational system and labour market institutions. The papers on Latin America and Southeast Asia emphasised the importance of educational policy. In Latin America education policy has been skewed, favouring urban middle classes, and has resulted in high levels of primary and tertiary education and low levels of secondary education. This has created a missing middle and a distorted labour supply, resulting in a mismatch between labour supply and growing demand for skilled workers, raising returns to education and skills and widening wage inequality. Labour market reforms have made matters worse. This contrasts with East Asia, where inequality fell during the period when growth was led by exports intensive in low-skilled labour, matched with a move towards universal primary education. This made generally available the skills necessary to participate in globalisation. In the 1990s in both regions, globalisation contributed to rising inequality because it created mismatches between increased demand for highly skilled labour and supply produced by the educational system. The extent to which this occurred varied across countries according to the degree of equality in their educational policies. For the most part, the lesson from the meeting was that the few middle-income countries that have successfully globalised — increasing their integration into the world economy while maintaining or improving inequality — have done so for one of two reasons. Either they had relatively equal asset distributions to begin with, or they had strong institutions that gave them, in Kindleberger's phrase, the capacity to transform themselves through investments in human and physical capital and other dynamic reallocations of resources.

The lessons from low-income countries in Africa were somewhat different and more tentative. With the exception of South Africa, these countries face a different world market niche, being largely commodity exporters, and have weak institutions, i.e. a limited capacity to transform. The few successful cases of globalisation — Uganda, Ghana, Mauritius — appear to have benefited heavily from favourable initial trends in world commodity prices for exports, and their relatively equal land distribution meant that these commodities were produced by smallholders. The success of Uganda and smallholder production of coffee stands in sharp contrast to the difficulties experienced in Zambia and state ownership of copper, the world price of which fell following the implementation of a broad reform package. Moreover, in the successful cases the opportunity afforded by favourable price trends and land ownership patterns was reinforced by policies supporting rural areas and some social welfare systems. (The latter usually benefited losers from reform who were not always the poor but provided crucial political support for continued reforms.) Taken together, this combination of policies engendered a virtuous circle of political support for further reform combined with external financial assistance, allowing pro-poor globalisation to continue even when key commodity prices weakened.

Policy Recommendations

For globalisation to contribute to alleviating rather than increasing poverty, more attention needs to be paid to *preparing vulnerable groups and the poorest countries to face increased competition successfully*. Growth is not sufficient. Recent research has shown that policy ideally should target redistributing assets or income, and that traditional concerns about negative trade-offs with growth or with problems of implementation or political feasibility are probably no less severe than those presented by market-oriented reforms[2]. The second-best alternative is to create greater access to productive resources and other supply-side policies, such as infrastructure investment in rural areas and agriculture, where most of the poor are found. This cannot be done naively. The correlation between extra spending and better outcomes is generally weak; quality and distribution are more important.

The speed and sequencing of external and domestic liberalisation relative to supply-side investments and institution building must be tailored to the particular circumstances of individual countries. The key determinant is the extent of a country's "transformation gap", i.e. the existence of distortions in the production structure and allocation of resources vs. the country's capacity to transform itself (to reallocate resources). Countries faced with large distortions, e.g. highly unequal asset distributions or weak transformative institutions, most likely need to liberalise more gradually and sequentially, placing greater emphasis on strengthening domestic governance and capacity building. On the other hand, some liberalisation, especially in the poorest countries, must proceed to provide opportunities for growth and redistribution. It is necessary to create a bigger pie to ease the political tensions caused by redistribution as well as create winners to provide political support for reform. In many countries, liberalisation can undermine corruption and cronyism, but in many cases liberalisation itself has given rise to new versions of these old problems where care was not taken to assure transparency and appropriate governance, for example the privatisation of state assets without increasing competition.

Successful globalisation requires *stronger transformative capacity* in the form of domestic institutions, particularly those involved in restructuring through investment and reallocation of resources — education and training, labour markets, financial markets, entrepreneurial capacity and infrastructure. Where these transformative institutions are weak, *capacity building is an essential pre-requisite* for sustainable, pro-poor globalisation. Capital account liberalisation and domestic financial market liberalisation are particularly demanding of strong domestic governance and institutions. When these conditions are lacking such liberalisation is premature. In many cases it has contributed to creating macroeconomic instability, greater inequality and all too often financial crises. Financial liberalisation in all its aspects needs to be the last step in any sequencing of liberalisation and needs to wait until the appropriate governance is in place. It is worth recalling that most OECD member countries did not liberalise their capital accounts until the late 1970s or even later.

114

The shift to a smaller role of the state and greater market provision of services and allocation of resources must be made with care. The state plays a key role in successful globalisation, and not simply in providing framework conditions. It must ensure proper governance of markets, especially in competition policy and transparency. As the experience of agriculture in several African countries has shown, *the state may need to continue to play a role where market institutions are weak or under development*. That role can include the provision of inputs or marketing of agricultural products or the provision of social services and a safety net.

Education, training and labour market policies are particularly important for equitable globalisation. They must target a more equal distribution of human capital. Education policy needs to target universal education and build from the bottom up, (primary first, then secondary, and tertiary last). While some tertiary education is important in filling in the human component of good governance and transformatiive institutions — i.e. ensuring an adequate supply of well trained teachers and civil servants — policy needs to avoid over-investing in higher education in an attempt to leapfrog stages of economic development. Educational investment needs to match the derived demand for labour skills based on a country's world market niche and comparative advantage. Again, this is not necessarily a function of extra spending — quality and equal access in terms of social class, geography and particularly gender are important. Providing financial incentives to poor families to cover the lost income from children who remain in school can be key; experimental programmes for this in Mexico (*Progresa*) and Brazil (*Borsa Escola*) have proven effective.

Labour-market flexibility is important to ensure that employment shifts in response to global markets occur smoothly. Labour-market reforms intended to increase flexibility are frequently associated with greater wage inequality, however, and need to be undertaken with extreme care. More research is needed on how to achieve balanced labour-market reform.

Changes in OECD policies are necessary to increase market access for developing country exports. Trade liberalisation and market access need to be more symmetrical between OECD and developing countries. OECD policies limiting agricultural and labour-intensive imports must be liberalised, preferably in conjunction with other policies permitting an orderly and rapid transition of OECD countries out of non-competitive agriculture and sectors intensive in unskilled labour.

Multilateral trade negotiations grant concessions based on equivalent dollar-for-dollar exchange of greater market access. This practice is inherently biased against developing countries with their smaller markets and demands sophisticated analytical expertise that they often lack, especially the least-developed (LDCs). Trade negotiations need to include explicitly the goal of improving development prospects, allowing developing countries not only long adjustment periods but time to maintain certain protectionist measures consistent with the development of new productive capacities, as was done by East Asian countries through most of the 1970s and mid-1980s. In fact the very success of these and a few other middle-income countries has increased the competition faced by those developing countries trying to follow, making special treatment all the more necessary.

The current structure of global governance has not kept pace with changes in the world economy and does not sufficiently promote development and poverty reduction. New modalities are necessary for global governance, emphasising participation of stakeholders and a rebalancing of political power in global institutions. The procedures, decision making and structures of a number of these institutions, especially the WTO and the Bretton Woods institutions, are not sufficiently inclusive of developing countries or of stakeholders from these countries. Much too often their critics are right. Their policies do not serve to promote development, and the costs of those policy failures are borne by the developing countries, particularly the most vulnerable parts of their populations. Greater inclusion, not just consultation, of developing country stakeholders in decision making and policy formation is essential for them to adopt explicitly pro-development policies tailored to the needs of individual countries and the poor within them. Policy mistakes and failures can not always be attributed to a failure of political will or implementation on the part of developing countries. Such errors are to be expected, as they would be with the lending of domestic financial institutions. As with domestic bankruptcy codes, a means must be found for more equitably distributing the costs of those failures, with international institutions assuming their share of both the responsibility and the financial burden.

Notes

1. For a recent summary, see Cornia and Kiiski (2001).

2. See Dagdeviren, van der Hoeven and Weeks (2001). The authors show that redistribution, or redistribution combined with growth, is the most direct and effective way to reduce poverty in most developing countries, except for the least developed, where incomes are too low for there to be anything to redistribute.

Bibliography

CHEN, S. and M. RAVALLION (1999) "How Did the World's Poorest Fare in the 1990s?", unprocessed, World Bank, Washington, D.C.

CORNIA, G.A. and S. KIISKI (2001), "Trends in Income Distribution in the Post World War II Period: Evidence and Interpretation", paper prepared for the WIDER Development Conference, *Growth and Poverty*. 25-26 May 2001, Helsinki.

DAGDEVIREN, H., R. VAN DER HOEVEN and J. WEEKS (2001), "Redistribution Does Matter: Growth and Redistribution for Poverty Reduction", paper presented at the WIDER Development Conference, *Growth and Poverty*, 25-26 May 2001, Helsinki.

DOLLAR, D. and A. KRAAY (2000), "Trade, Growth and Poverty", paper prepared for the Conference on Poverty and the International Economy, Stockholm, Sweden, sponsored by the World Bank, William Davidson Institute, Swedish Ministry of Foreign Affairs and The Parliamentary Commission on Swedish Policy for Global Development, 20-21 October.

KOHL, R. and K.H. O'ROURKE (2000), "What's New About Globalisation: Implications for Income Inequality in Developing Countries", paper presented at the Conference on Poverty and Inequality in Developing Countries: A Policy Dialogue on the Effects of Globalisation, 30 November-1 December 2000, OECD Development Centre, Paris.

WOOD, A. (1997) "Openness and Wage Inequality in Developing Countries: the Latin American Challenge to East Asian Conventional Wisdom", *World Bank Economic Review* 11(1).

WOOD, A. (1994), *North-South Trade, Employment and Inequality*, Clarendon Press, Oxford.

APPENDICES

POVERTY AND INCOME INEQUALITY IN DEVELOPING COUNTRIES:
A POLICY DIALOGUE ON THE EFFECTS OF GLOBALISATION

30 NOVEMBER - 1 DECEMBER 2000

Appendix I
Programme

**Poverty and Income Inequality in Developing Countries:
A Policy Dialogue on the Effects of Globalisation**

Organised by the OECD Development Centre
with the support of the Ford Foundation and the World Bank Institute
(and in co-operation with the Carnegie Endowment for International Peace, the
Gulbenkian Foundation, UNDP, UNU/WIDER, IDB and CEDERS/Université de la
Méditerranée/Aix-Marseille II)

Thursday, 30 November

Welcoming Remarks: Jorge BRAGA DE MACEDO, President, OECD Development Centre

Session I. International Trends in Income Distribution

Moderator: Richard KOHL, Senior Economist and Project Manager, OECD
Development Centre

Presentations:
"Decomposing Changes in Income Inequality in Emerging Market Economies"
François BOURGUIGNON, Professor of Economics, *École des Hautes Etudes en Sciences
Sociales*, DELTA (Department of Theoretical and Applied Economics), Paris and World
Bank, Washington

"Trends in Income Inequality in OECD Member Countries"
Mark PEARSON, Senior Economist, Directorate for Education, Employment, Labour
and Social Affairs, OECD

Discussants: Tony ATKINSON, Warden of Nuffield College, Oxford, UK
Giovanni Andrea CORNIA, Special Adviser for Research, UNICEF and
University of Florence

Open Discussion

Session II. The Relationship between Globalisation and National Income Inequality

Moderator: Jorge BRAGA DE MACEDO, President, OECD Development Centre

Presentations:
"What's New About Globalisation: Implications for Income Inequality in Developing Countries"
    Richard KOHL, Senior Economist and Project Manager, OECD Development Centre
    Kevin H. O'ROURKE, Professor, Department of Economics, Trinity College, Dublin
"The Impact of Globalisation on the Labour Share of National Income"
    Ishac DIWAN, Manager, Economic Policy for Poverty Reduction Division, World Bank Institute

Discussants: James GALBRAITH, Professor, Lyndon B. Johnson School of Public Affairs, University of Texas, Austin
John ROBERTS, Department for International Development, UK

Open Discussion

Session III. Regional Breakout Session

Session III.A. Explaining the Cross-Country Variance in the Social Impact of Globalisation: Endowment, Integration or Policy Response?

Latin America

Moderator:	Albert FISHLOW, Senior Partner, Violy, Byorum and Partners and Visiting Professor, School of International and Public Affairs, Columbia University (formerly with the U.S. Council on Foreign Relations)
Paper Presentations:	Samuel MORLEY, Visiting Research Fellow, International Food Policy Research Institute (IFPRI), Washington, D.C. Miguel SZEKELY, Research Economist, Research Department, Inter-American Development Bank
Testimony from Civil Society:	Néstor CALLEGARI, Argentine Federation of Electricity Workers, Argentina Victor SUAREZ, National Association of Peasant Enterprises (agricultural co-operatives), Mexico Antonio WERNA DE SALVO, National Confederation of Agriculture, Brazil
Rapporteur:	Barbara STALLINGS, Director, Economic Development Division, UN Economic Commission for Latin America and the Caribbean, Santiago, Chile

East Asia

Moderator:	Shoji NISHIMOTO, Director, Strategy and Policy Department, Asian Development Bank, Manila, Philippines
Paper Presentations:	Mari PANGESTU, Board Member, Centre for Strategic and International Studies (CSIS), Jakarta, Indonesia
Testimony from Civil Society:	Mokhtar PAKPAHAN, SBSI (trade union), Indonesia Ravadee PRASERTCHAROENSUK, Thai NGO-COD, Thailand Ernesto ARELLANO, National Federation of Labour; National Confederation of Labour; International Federation of Building and Wood Workers, Philippines
Rapporteur:	S. Mansoob MURSHED, UN University/WIDER, Helsinki, Finland

Africa

Moderator:	Gun Britt ANDERSSON, State Secretary for Development Co-operation, Migration and Asylum Policy, Sweden
Paper Presentations:	Steve KAYIZZI-MUGERWA, Associate Professor, Göteburg University and Project Director, UN University/WIDER, Helsinki, Finland
Testimony from Civil Society:	Victoria SEBAGERIKA, Uganda National Farmers Association, Uganda Antonio de BARROS AGUIAR, National Chamber of Commerce, Sao Tomé Soukeyna NDIAYE BA, Femme, Développement, Entreprise en Afrique, Senegal
Rapporteur:	Daniel COHEN, Professor, Ecole Normale Supérieure, Paris and Special Adviser, OECD Development Centre

Session III.B. Comparing Countries' Policy Responses to Globalisation

Latin America

Moderator:	Albert FISHLOW, Senior Partner, Violy, Byorum and Partners and Visiting Professor, School of International and Public Affairs, Columbia University (formerly with the U.S. Council on Foreign Relations)
Paper Presentation:	James ROBINSON, Professor, Department of Political Science, University of California at Berkeley, California, USA
Policy Maker:	Official from the Ministry of Social Affairs, Mexico

Testimony from Civil Society: Jorge Cardelli, Director, 'Escuela Marina Vilte', CTERA (Education Workers' Confederation), Argentina
Alberto Gomez-Flores, UNORCA (farmers' association), Mexico
Jorge Mattoso, Adviser of Workers Party and former researcher of DIEESE (Trade Union Research Centre), Brazil,

Rapporteur: Barbara Stallings, Director, Economic Development Division, UN Economic Commission for Latin America and the Caribbean, Santiago, Chile

East Asia

Moderator: Shoji Nishimoto, Director, Strategy and Policy Department, Asian Development Bank, Manila, Philippines

Paper Presentation: K.S. Jomo, Professor, Applied Economics Department, University of Malaya

Policy Maker: Mekvichai Banasopit, Former Deputy Governor, Bangkok, Thailand

Testimony from Civil Society: Thuraisingham Indrani, SEA Food Security Council, Malaysia
Leonardo Montemayor, Federation of Free Farmers and Member of Parliament, Philippines
Lisa Isa, Former Secretary-General of FOKUBA, Indonesia

Rapporteur: S. Mansoob Murshed, UN University/WIDER, Helsinki, Finland

Africa

Moderator: Gun Britt Andersson, State Secretary for Development Co-operation, Migration and Asylum Policy, Sweden

Paper Presentation: Yvonne M. Tsikata, Senior Research Fellow, Economic and Social Research Foundation, Dar es Salaam, Tanzania

Policy Maker: Elyett Rasendratsiforo, Former Minister of Tourism, Madagascar

Testimony from Civil Society: Thomas Bediako, Education International, Togo
Maggie Kigozi, Uganda Investment Authority, Uganda
Ebrahim-Khalil Hassen, National Labour and Economic Development Institute (NALEDI), South Africa

Rapporteur: Daniel Cohen, Professor, Ecole Normale Supérieure, Paris and Special Adviser, OECD Development Centre

Friday, 1 December

Session IV: Comparing Regional Experiences: The Effects of and Policy Response to Globalisation

Moderator:	Richard KOHL, Senior Economist and Project Manager, OECD Development Centre

Rapporteurs' Reports:

Latin America:	Barbara STALLINGS, Director, Economic Development Division, UN Economic Commission for Latin America and the Caribbean, Santiago, Chile
East Asia:	Mansoob MURSHED, UN University/WIDER, Helsinki, Finland
Africa:	Daniel COHEN, Professor, Ecole Normale Supérieure, Paris and Special Adviser, OECD Development Centre

Open Discussion

Session V: Policy Recommendations: Where Do We Go From Here?

Moderator:	Jorge BRAGA DE MACEDO, President, OECD Development Centre

Synthesis:
"Lessons from Country and Regional Experience"
    Richard KOHL, Senior Economist and Project Manager, OECD Development Centre

Comments:	Dani RODRIK, Professor, Harvard University
	Emmanuel TUMUSIIME MUTEBILE, Permanent Secretary, Ministry of Finance, Uganda
	José Pablo ARELLANO, Former Minister of Education, Chile

Open Discussion

Conclusions:	Jorge BRAGA DE MACEDO, President, OECD Development Centre

Appendix II
List of Papers Presented at the Dialogue

"Distribution and Growth in Latin America in an Era of Structural Reform", by Samuel Morley, Visiting Research Fellow, IFPRI.

"Economic Reform and Wage Differentials in Latin America", by Miguel Szekely, Research Economist, IDB.

"Globalisation and Income Inequality in Uganda", by Arne Bigsten, Professor, Department of Economics, University of Gothenburg, Sweden.

"Globalisation and Inequality in South Africa", by Nicoli Jean Nattrass, Professor, University of Cape Town, and Jeremy Seekings, University of Cape Town.

"Globalisation and Inequality: The Case of Argentina", by Ricardo Bebczuk, Senior Researcher, Universidad Nacional de La Plata, and Leonardi Gasparini, Senior Researcher, Universidad Nacional de La Plata.

"Globalisation, Economic Policy and Equity: The Case of Malaysia", by Fauziah Abu Hasan.

"Globalisation, Growth and Income Inequality: A Review of the African Experience", by Steve Kayizzi-Mugerwa, Associate Professor, Göteburg University and Project Director, UNU/WIDER.

"Globalisation, Liberalisation, Poverty and Income Inequality in Southeast Asia", by K.S. Jomo, Professor, University of Malaya.

"Globalisation, Poverty and Inequality in Zambia during the 1990s", by Neil McCulloch, Bob Baulch and Milasoa Cherel-Robson.

"Globalization and Endogenous Educational Responses: The Main Economic Transition Channels", by François Bourguignon, Professor of Economics, EHESS, DELTA, Paris and World Bank, and Thierry Verdier, DELTA, Paris.

"Globalization, Poverty and Inequality in Indonesia", by Tubagus Feridhabusetyawan, Senior Economist and Deputy Director of Research, CSIS.

"Globalization, Poverty and Inequality in Sub-Saharan Africa: a Political Economy Appraisal", by Yvonne Tsikata, Senior Research Fellow, Economic and Social Research Foundation, Dar es Salaam, Tanzania.

"Income Distribution in OECD Countries", by Mark Pearson, Senior Economist, Directorate for Education, Employment, Labour and Social Affairs, OECD.

"Labour Share and Globalisation", by Ishac Diwan, Manager, Economic Policy for Poverty Reduction Division, World Bank Institute, Washington, D.C.

"Poverty and Inequality: The Case of Thailand", by Pasuk Phongpaichit, Professor, Chulalongkorn University, Chiang Mai University and Sarntisart Isra.

"Social Impact of Globalisation in Southeast Asia", by Mari Pangestu, Board Member, CSIS.

"What's New About Globalisation: Implications for Income Inequality in Developing Countries", by Richard Kohl, Senior Economist, OECD Development Centre and Kevin O'Rourke, Professor, Trinity College, Dublin.

"Where Does Inequality Come From? Ideas and Implications for Latin America", by James Robinson, Professor, University of California at Berkeley.

Appendix III
List of Participants in the Dialogue

Authors, Experts and Discussants

José Pablo ARELLANO MARIN	Former Minister of Education of Chile, Santiago
Tony ATKINSON	Warden of Nuffield College, Oxford
Ricardo Néstor BEBCZUK	Senior Researcher, Economics Department, Universidad Nacional de La Plata, Argentina
Arne BIGSTEN	Professor, Department of Economics, University of Gothenburg, Sweden
François BOURGUIGNON	Professor of Economics, École des Hautes Etudes en Sciences Sociales, DELTA (Department of Theoretical and Applied Economics), Paris and World Bank, Washington, D.C.
Jorge BRAGA DE MACEDO	President, OECD Development Centre, Paris
Daniel COHEN	Professor, École Normale Supérieure, Paris and Special Adviser, OECD Development Centre, Paris
Giovanni Andrea CORNIA	Special Adviser for Research, UNICEF, and University of Florence
Ishac DIWAN	Manager, Economic Policy for Poverty Reduction Division, World Bank Institute, Washington, D.C.
Tubagus FERIDHANUSETYAWAN	Senior Economist and Deputy Director of Research, Centre for Strategic and International Studies (CSIS), Jakarta
Albert FISHLOW	Senior Partner, Violy, Byorum and Partners, and Visiting Professor SIPA (School of International and Public Affairs), Columbia University, New York (formerly with the US Council on Foreign Relations)
James GALBRAITH	Professor, LBJ School of Public Affairs, University of Texas-Austin
K.S. JOMO	Professor, Applied Economics Department, University of Malaya, Kuala Lumpur
Steve KAYIZZI-MUGERWA	Associate Professor, Göteburg University and Project Director, UN University/WIDER, Helsinki
Richard KOHL	Senior Economist and Project Manager, OECD Development Centre, Paris
Katherine McFATE	Rockefeller Foundation, New York
Manuel "Butch" MONTES	Ford Foundation, New York
Samuel MORLEY	Visiting Research Fellow, International Food Policy Research Institute (IFPRI), Washington, D.C.
Mary MUDUULI	Ministry of Finance, Planning and Economic Development, Kampala

S. Mansoob Murshed	UNU/WIDER, Helsinki
Nicoli Jean Nattrass	Professor, School of Economics, University of Cape Town
Shoji Nishimoto	Director, Strategy and Policy Department, Asian Development Bank, Manila
Neil McCulloch	IDS, University of Sussex
Kevin H. O'Rourke	Professor, Department of Economics, Trinity College, Dublin
Mari Pangestu	Board Member, Centre for Strategic and International Studies (CSIS), Jakarta
Mark Pearson	Senior Economist, Directorate for Education, Employment, Labour and Social Affairs, OECD, Paris
John Roberts	Department for International Development (DFID), London
James Robinson	Professor, Department of Political Science, University of California at Berkeley
Dani Rodrik	Professor, Harvard University, Cambridge, MA
Barbara Stallings	Director, Economic Development Division, UN Economic Commission for Latin America and the Caribbean, Santiago
Miguel Szekely	Research Economist, Research Department, Inter-American Development Bank, Washington, D.C.
Yvonne Tsikata	Senior Research Fellow, Economic and Social Research Foundation, Dar es Salaam
Emmanuel Tumusiime Mutebile	Permanent Secretary, Ministry of Finance, Planning and Economic Development, Kampala
Thierry Verdier	DELTA, Paris

Civil Society Representatives

AFRICA

Antonio Barros Aguiar	National Chamber of Commerce, Sao Tomé e Principe
Soukeyna Ndiaye Ba	Femme, Développement, Entreprise en Afrique, Senegal
Najib Balala	National Chamber of Commerce and Industry, Kenya
Thomas Bediako	Education International, Lome, Togo
Martha J.N. Bitwale	Tanzanian Women Miners Association, Tanzania
Maria do Carmo Nascimento	President, ASSOMEL, Angola
Lawrence Egulu	ICFTU African Regional Organisation (AFRO), Kenya
Mariatou Guiehoa	Second Deputy Secretary General, Union Générale des Travailleurs de Côte d'Ivoire
Ebrahim-Khalil Hassen	National Labour and Economic Development Institute (Naledi), South Africa
Charles Kabuga	Head of IFAP Developing Country Activities, Paris
Maggie Kigozi	Uganda Investment Authority
Philip Kiriro	(IFAP), Kenya
Sarah Kitakule	Uganda Women Entrepreneurs Association

J.R.L KUTSOKOANE	Executive Director, National Africa Farmer's Union, South Africa
Solly MABUSELA	South African Democratic Teachers' Union
Neva MAKGETLA	COSATU, South Africa
Pedro Joaquim MANJAZE	Secretary for International Relations, Organisation of Mozambican Workers, Maputo
John MOHOELE	South African NGO Coalition SANGOCO
Maria do Carmo NASCIMENTO	President, Association of Business Women of Luanda, Angola
Lucia QUACHEY	Ghanaian Association of Women Entrepreneurs (GAWE)
Jack RAATH	Agri South Africa (IFAP), South Africa
Elyett RASENDRATSIFORO	Former Cabinet Secretary, Minister of Tourism; Women and Business, Antananarivo, Madagascar
Victoria SEBAGERIKA	Uganda National Farmers Association (IFAP)
Bayi SINIBAGUY-MOLLET	President, CLONG-CONGO and Co-ordinator ROSAC (Réseau des organisations de la société civile d'Afrique centrale) Brazzaville

LATIN AMERICA

Carlos ABICALIL	Teachers Union CNTE, Brasilia
Josefina ARANDA BEZAURY	Small Coffee Grain Producers, Oaxaca, Mexico
Néstor CALLEGARI	Argentine Federation of Electricity Workers
Jorge CARDELLI	Confederation of Education Workers (CTERA), Argentina
Isabel CRUZ	AMUCSS (Asoc. Mex. de Uniones de Crédito del Sector Social), Mexico
Alejandro DELFINO	Vice-President of IFAP, Sociedad Rural Argentina
Alvaro FIALLOS	UNAG, Nicaragua
Alberto GOMEZ FLORES	UNORCA, Mexico
Jorge MATTOSO	Center of Trade Union Studies and Labor Economics, University of Caminos, Brazil
Jorge NAHUEL	Indigenous group "Coordinadora Mapuche de Neuquen", Argentina
German RODRIGUEZ CAMPOS	El Surco, Chile
Victor SUAREZ	National Association of Peasant Enterprises, Mexico
Antonio VILLALBA	FAT and Mexican Net Against Free Trade
Antonio E. WERNA DE SALVO	President, Confederação Nacional de Agricultura, Brasilia

ASIA

Ernesto ARELLANO	National Federation of Labour, Philippines
Ibrahim Ahmad BAJUNID	General Secretary, Malaysian Association for Education, Kuala Lumpur
Silam HASSAN	Chairperson Women's Committee, Malaysian Trades Union Congress
Lisa ISA	Former General Secretary of FOKUBA, Indonesia

Banasopit MEKVICHAI	Former Deputy Governor, Bangkok, Thailand
Leonardo MONTEMAYOR	Federation of Free Farmers (IFAP), Philippines
Mokhtar PAKPAHAN	Trade Union Leader SBSI, Indonesia
Ravadee PRASERTCHAROENSUK	Secretary-General of the NGO Coordinating Committee on Development (NGO-COD), Thailand
Bismo SANYOTO	International Department, SBSI, Jakarta
Indrani THURAISINGHAM	SEA Food Security Council, Malaysia

Other Participants

Mohsen BEN CHIBANI	Economist, International Confederation of Free Trade Unions (IFCTU), Brussels
M.H. BEN YAICHE	La Vie Economique, Paris
Michèle BERNARD-ROYER	Valeurs Vertes, Paris
William BRANSON	Consultant, World Bank and Visiting Fellow, OECD Development Centre, Paris
Sian BUCKLEY	TVE, UK
Denis COGNEAU	DIAL-IRD, France
Kjetil ELSEBUTANGEN	
Juan FLORES	
Michael GRIMM	DIAL and Institut d'Etudes Politiques de Paris
Charlotte GUENARD	DIAL, Paris
Gabriela GUERRERO	ISS, The Netherlands
Javier HERRERA	Chargé de Recherche, Institut de Recherche pour le Développement, DIAL, Paris
John HUMPHREY	Programme Director, IDS, Sussex
Denis JACQUOT	CFDT, Paris
Ethan B. KAPSTEIN	Stassen Professor of International Peace at the University of Minnesota, Visiting Professor, INSEAD and Visiting Professor, IFRI
Peeter-Jaan KASK	LO-Tidningen, Trade Union Weekly Journal, Sweden
Cho KHONG	Chief Political Analyst PXG, Shell International Limited, London
David KING	IFAP, Paris
Robert LAMB	Director, TVE, UK
Maricarmen MARTINEZ	
Mohamed Ali MAROUANI	DIAL, European Centre of Research in Development Economics, Paris
Natalie MISALJEVICH	TVE, UK
Agnés RAVOYARD	Rédacteur en Chef, Galaxie Production, Paris
Mireille RAZAFINDRAKOTO	DIAL, Centre de recherche européen en economie du développement, Paris
Gerardo David ROSAS	Dial/Team, Paris
Alice SINDZINGRE	Centre National de la Recherche Scientifique, Paris

Luciana UCHOA	BBC Brazilian Service, Paris
Andrew WALKER	Economics Correspondent, BBC World Service, London
Alan WINTERS	University of Sussex
Gregg Pascal ZACHARY	Wall Street Journal

Diplomatic Corps (including national delegations to the OECD)

Argentina

Nelson MARTIN	First Secretary, Embassy of Argentina in France – Department of Economics

Austria

Karin REINPRECHT	Federal Ministry for Foreign Affairs

Belgium

Paul FRIX	Permanent Deputy Representative to the OECD

Brazil

Adalnio GANEM	Minister-Counsellor, Embassy of Brazil
Lauro Eduardo SOUTELLO-ALVES	Head of the OECD Liaison Section, Embassy of Brazil

Canada

Patricia MALIKAIL	Deputy Director, Economic Relations with Developing Countries Division, Department of Foreign Affairs and International Trade

Chile

Claudio ROJAS	Head of OECD Department, Ministry of Foreign Affairs, Santiago
Marcelo GARCIA	Representative of Chile to the OECD Development Centre

China (People's Republic of)

Deyun MA	First Secretary, Embassy of the Popular Republic of China, Paris
Tiecheng HAN	Minister Counsellor, Embassy of the Popular Republic of China, Paris

Czech Republic

Lenka ADAMCOVA	Faculty of International Relations, High School of Economics, Prague

Denmark

Anya Riber SKYDT	Policy and Planning Department, South Group, Danish Ministry of Foreign Affairs

Finland

Eija LIMNELL	Counsellor, Permanent Delegation of Finland to the OECD

France

Jean-Pierre CLING	Ministry of Economy, Finance and Industry
Patrick ALLARD	Ministry of Foreign Affairs

Germany

Wolfgang BICHMANN	Kreditanstalt für Wiederaufbau, Frankfurt
Susanne RIETSCHEL	Permanent Delegation of Germany to the OECD
Eduard WESTREICHER	Counsellor, Permanent Delegation of Germany to the OECD

Hungary

Ambassador Prof. Dr. Bela KADAR Permanent Representative to the OECD

Italy

Guido LA TELLA	Permanant Delgation of Italy to the OECD
Luisa BOARETTO	Trainee, Permanant Delgation of Italy to the OECD

Japan

Katsuhiko NAKADATE	Assistant Director, Operations Strategy Division, Development Assistance Strategy, Japan Bank for International Cooperation (JBIC)
Naoya OCHI	JBIC Paris Office
Tomoko ONUKI	Permanent Delegation of Japan to the OECD

Mexico

Magdalena DIAZ	Third Secretary, Permanent Delegation of Mexico to the OECD

Netherlands

Paul SCIARONE	Deputy Permanent Representative of the Netherlands to the OECD

Norway

Marit M. STRAND	NORAD

Poland

Jan BIELAWSKI	Ministry of Foreign Affairs
Ryszard PIASECKI	Ministry of Foreign Affairs
Ryszard RYSINSKI	Counsellor, Permanent Delegation of Poland to the OECD

Portugal

Ambassador Jorge DE LEMOS GODINHO Permanent Representative of Portugal to the OECD

Irene PAREDES	Counsellor, Permanent Delegation of Portugal to the OECD

Sweden

Torgny HOLMGREN	Ministry of Foreign Affairs, Sweden
Mia HORN AF RANTZIEN	Stockholm School of Economics
Tove STRAUSS	Stockholm School of Economics
Pernilla JOSEFSSON	Permanent Delegation of Sweden to the OECD

Switzerland

Hugo BRUGGMAN	Federal Department of Economy
Paul OBRIST	Permanent Delegation of Switzerland to the OECD

Turkey

Emel CEVIKOZ	Expert, Turkish Cooperation and Development Agency (TIKA)

United Kingdom

Martin ROPER	Permanent Delegation of the United Kingdom to the OECD

International Monetary Fund

S. Erik OPPERS, Economist

Sergio PEREIRA LEITE, Assistant Director, IMF Office in Europe

World Health Organisation

Nick DRAGER

David WOODWARD

OECD Secretariat*

Sally SHELTON-COLBY, Deputy Secretary-General, OECD

Richard CAREY, Development Co-operation Directorate (DCD)

Dag EHRENPREIS, Senior Advisor for Poverty Reduction, DCD

Paul ISENMAN, Head of Division, DCD

Frans LAMMERSEN, Principal Administrator, DCD

Jean-Claude FAURE, Chair, Development Assistance Committee

Thomas HATZICHRONOGLOU, Principal Administrator, DSTI/EAS

Jean-Marie METZGER, Director, Trade Directorate

Thai-Thanh DANG, Administrator Income Distribution, ECO/PSRA

Robert VALLETTA, Consultant, ELS/EAP

Brendan GILLESPIE, Head of Branch, Environment/NMC

Paul PARADIS, Public Affairs (PAC/AFF)

John WEST, Head of Division, PAC/AFF

Elisabeth THIOLERON, Club du Sahel

OECD Development Centre*

Ulrich HIEMENZ, Director for Co-ordination

Kiichiro FUKASAKU, Head of Division (Integration of Developing Countries into the World Trading System)

Charles OMAN, Principal Administrator, Corporate Governance

Catherine DUPORT, Head of Administration and Support Services

Colm FOY, Head of Communication

Henny HELMICH, Head of External Co-operation

Kristen NEYMARC, Secretary of the Advisory Board

Myriam ANDRIEUX

Marsha BEAUDOIN

Federico BONAGLIA

Maurizio BUSSOLO

Claire BUSTARRET

Laurie CHAMBERLAIN

Antje FIEHN

Martin Grandes

Roberto LONGO

Pamela MARQUEYROL

Ida McDONNELL

Sandrine SABATIER

Morag SORANNA

Marcelo SOTO

Jorge VELAZQUEZ

Terri WELLS

* Except those listed as authors or discussants

OECD PUBLICATIONS, 2, rue André-Pascal, 75775 PARIS CEDEX 16
PRINTED IN FRANCE
(41 2003 04 1 P) ISBN 92-64-10187-X – No. 53083 2003